Take a Bible Break

TAKE
A
BIBLE
BREAK

by

W. E. McCumber

Beacon Hill Press of Kansas City
Kansas City, Missouri

Copyright 1986
by Beacon Hill Press of Kansas City

ISBN: 083-411-0806

Printed in the
United States of America

Cover art: Crandall Vail

10 9 8 7 6 5 4 3 2

Dedicated to a cherished friend,
Dan Cheshine,
who long has known the value of the Bible
and of brevity.

Contents

Preface

Coffee breaks and Coke breaks are a way of life in the United States, just as breaks for tea have been in England for a long time.

How enriched our lives would be if we all took Bible breaks each day! A few moments spent in reading and reflecting upon a passage of Scripture, in listening and talking to the Lord, would bring elements of love, faith, peace, and strength to all our relationships in life.

In this little book you will find some guided Bible breaks. They encompass a variety of themes and address a variety of needs. They speak to Christians and to non-Christians—and to those who think they are Christians but are not. Their truths are simply and plainly stated. Each one closes with a short, sincere prayer. Use them, along with your Bible, and they will do you good.

I have used the King James Version of the Bible, taking the liberty of paraphrasing slightly to bring verb forms and pronoun forms into agreement with today's usage. For an interesting and helpful comparison, you may enjoy reading the passages selected in a newer translation.

May the God of all grace make His Word and this book a means of blessing to you!

W. E. McCumber

God's Surprises

Have you had any strange dreams lately? Dreams are intriguing. Their causes can range from too much pizza to God. That's right—God can speak to people in their dreams. One man who experienced such a dream was Jacob. Get your Bible and let's read about it. The story is found in Gen. 28:11-22. We want to focus on verses 12 and 13:

> And he dreamed, and behold a ladder set up on the earth, and the top of it reached to heaven: and behold the angels of God ascending and descending on it. And, behold, the Lord stood above it, and said, I am the Lord God of Abraham your father, and the God of Isaac: the land whereon you lie, to you will I give it, and to your seed.

Underline the "behold" phrases and let's discuss them for a few minutes.

_I-_ **"Behold a ladder"—here is a surprising union.** Heaven and earth were joined. God was in touch with man. And Jacob was learning that the connection could be made anytime, anywhere. Not just back home, where Papa Isaac and Mama Rebekah prayed around the family altar, but also amid the rocks and sand of the desert.

Jacob could not reach God, but God could reach him. Jacob had no ladder for climbing up to heaven. His works could never gain him access to God. But God had a ladder for reaching down to earth. He made the linkup on His own initiative. He is the God who is gracious to sinners.

The ladder still stands. *The name of the ladder is Jesus.* To one of His first disciples Jesus said, "Verily, verily, I say unto you, Hereafter you shall see heaven open, and the angels of God ascending and descending upon the Son of man" (John 1:51). Jesus is the union between God and man. No man comes to the Father except by Him. "There is one God, and one mediator between God and men, the man Christ Jesus" (1 Tim. 2:5).

II- "Behold the angels"—here is a surprising traffic. Jacob saw them going up and down the ladder. It wasn't a matter of fun and games. They were not taking physical therapy or doing calisthenics. Those angels were God's messengers. They were operating a delivery service, bringing the blessings of God down to the lives of men.

The New Testament tells us that angels are "ministering spirits" who minister to the "heirs of salvation" (Heb. 1:14). God was letting Jacob know that His delivery service reached the fringe areas and operated in hard times. Jacob didn't have to be snug in the family nest to get help from God. Anywhere, anytime, the messengers of mercy could reach him. Wherever you are, God has your address. He can reach you in His love and with His help, from New York's ghetto to Australia's outback.

III- "Behold the Lord"—here is a surprising presence. Why should the Lord be with Jacob? Jacob was on the lam to keep his brother, Esau, from killing him. Jacob was a crook from head to heels, a con man who had victimized his own family. That is lower than a grub worm's instep! And yet, here was God, full of promises to such an undeserving sinner!

God is merciful, and we are grateful for that. We are no better than Jacob. Some of us are just less successful in our schemes. "All have sinned" (Rom. 3:23), and our only hope is the mercy of God.

God is faithful. Just listen to His promise to Jacob: "Behold, I am with you, and will keep you in all places whither you go" (v. 15). He is a covenant-keeping, promise-fulfilling

God. *He never lets us go and never lets us down.* That is all the security anyone needs for the future! Hallelujah! With that kind of promise to lean on you can cancel any nervous breakdown you may have scheduled.

David Livingstone was alone, sick, and discouraged in the jungles of Africa. He was tempted to abandon his work as a missionary-explorer and return to England. But the words of Jesus Christ, "Lo, I am with you always" (Matt. 28:20), buoyed his heart to persevere. We are never alone! Whatever our circumstances, the Lord is there to save and help.

Jacob got so excited it woke him up. He said, "Surely the Lord is in this place" (v. 16), and he named it Bethel. Is there a Bethel in your life?

"Behold a ladder," "behold the angels," "behold the Lord." God's great surprises! To beat that, friend, you have to come over to the Gospels and see John the Baptist point to Jesus and hear him say, "Behold the Lamb of God" (John 1:29).

O God, we thank You for Your love and for Your ladder. Keep the angels coming. We cannot make it without Your forgiveness and blessings. And in response we will confess You as our God and honor You with our substance. In Jesus' name. Amen.

Life or Death

Have you made any tracks in the Old Testament lately? It's a shame the way we neglect what our fathers called "the Old Bible." It is a wealth of truth for the Church today, and without it we cannot begin to understand the New Testament.

So let's look at an Old Testament passage today. Read Deuteronomy 30. This is part of Moses' last speech to Israel, and he closes the speech with an impassioned plea for his people to be true to God. That is a common concern with the older generation, and history shows plenty of reasons for that concern. Note verse 19:

> I call heaven and earth to record this day against you, that I have set before you life and death, blessing and cursing: therefore choose life, that both you and your seed may live.

Whenever the Word of God is preached, those who hear it are facing life or death. Our response to the word that God speaks is a life-or-death matter. Moses was not a courthouse politician simply blowing off steam. He was God's spokesman, declaring God's Word, and human destiny was the issue. His words raise three pertinent questions.

I - **What is life?** Lots of people are dead and don't know it. The Bible speaks of those who are dead while they live. Just what is life?

The answer is right here in verse 20: "For he is your life." *Life is fellowship with God; all else is mere existence.* The Lord Jesus taught the same thing, saying, "This is life eternal, that

14

they might know you, the only true God, and Jesus Christ, whom you have sent" (John 17:3). Life is knowing God—not knowing about Him, the way a scientist knows about a white rat, but knowing Him as a friend knows a friend.

Look again at verse 20. Three words tell us what it means to know God and to have life. They are "love," "obey," and "cleave." Love God, obey His voice, and cleave to Him through thick and thin—do this and you will live joyfully and eternally.

Life is blessing. Compared to fellowship with God, Barnum and Bailey's circus is a three-ring bore. He is the God of endless surprises, the God of answered prayers, the God of mighty conquests. Walking with God is sheer adventure, a heady mixture of sacrifice and reward, of danger and fun. Fellowship with God in Christ—that is life!

II — **And what is death?** Death is the absence of life. *Death is alienation from God.*

Verse 17 puts it to us bluntly and clearly: "But if your heart turn away, so that you will not hear, but shall be drawn away, and worship other gods, and serve them . . . you shall surely perish." Death is turning away from God, refusing to obey His Word, and putting false gods in His place. Those gods are whatever your heart is drawn to first, whatever has priority in your life. Your idol may be your family, or even the family car. It may be your job, your house, or your television set. If the true God does not have first place in your life, your life-style can become your death rattle.

III — **What makes life possible and death avoidable?** After all, the human heart is wicked and idol-prone. Man cannot be expected to love God wholeheartedly. That is true, too sadly true. But go back to the great promise in verse 6: "And the Lord your God will circumcise your heart, and the heart of your seed, to love the Lord your God with all your heart, and with all your soul, that you may live."

Heart surgery! That is God's answer to man's need. Circumcision was an external sign of the covenant, God's agreement to be Israel's God, and Israel's agreement to be His people. But that ceremonial operation had no more real power to convey life than does a face-lift. Idols are born in the heart. Death begins in the heart. Life is lived from the inside out. The heart must be changed by God's power, and then we can love, obey, and cleave to Him.

God cleanses the heart from sin and fills it with His Spirit. Then the word of the covenant is written inwardly, and it has a power to create love and energize obedience. *Heart religion is life; all other religion is death.*

"Choose life." It will not be forced upon you, but it is offered to you. For your sake, and for your children's sake, "choose life."

O God, come to our hearts today with life-giving, life-cleansing, life-empowering grace. Help us to hear and live. Save us, for Jesus' sake, from all our sins and idols! Amen.

Why Read the Bible?

Let's not just read the Bible today, let's talk about why we read it. In God's sight motive counts for more than action. Jesus reproved the Pharisees for doing good things for bad reasons, such as praying to be heard of men and giving alms to be praised by men. Read the first psalm, which describes the blessed man, and mark verse 2:

> But his delight is in the law of the Lord; and in his law does he meditate day and night.

Law ("torah") is more than statutes, more than Ten Commandments. It means "teaching"—all that God says in order to save our souls and direct our lives. For us, it's the whole Bible, and it should have a place in our thinking day and night.

I– **Some read the Bible superstitiously.** Just as an apple a day is supposed to keep the doctor away, they seem to think a chapter a day keeps the devil away. So they read a prescribed amount, not meditating on it, not listening to it, not applying it to their lives, just skimming through it to get it over with.

It's true that the Bible is a defense against evil. Verse 1 implies this fact. But that's only true when we read with understanding and obey with tenacity. Otherwise, we might as well resort to a rabbit's foot or a four-leaf clover.

II– **Some read the Bible dutifully.** They don't desire it, they don't delight in it, but it's something Christian people ought to do, so they grudgingly do it. They resolve to do it, and they set out with fierce determination and patient resignation to do it. Very few of them keep it up.

Duty is a powerful impulse. It has sparked some heroic feats, some inspiring sacrifices. But like the Psalmist, the Lord's people ought to find the Lord's Word a delight. He said it is "sweeter than honey" (Ps. 19:10). Nobody eats honey as a matter of grim duty! No youngster chews bubble gum or eats candy bars because he has to!

III- **Some read the Bible critically.** They look for faults. They pore over the Bible in a determined search for errors, contradictions, and discrepancies. When they think they have spotted some, they catalogue and publicize them with glee. They are like fools who eat the bones and discard the fish.

Their arrogance is their destruction. They have made themselves judges of the Word, refusing to allow the Word to judge them. They will spend hours, even years, in close attendance upon Scripture without personal spiritual benefits. They collect nuts and bolts and scraps, but they never make anything positive and useful. Junkyard scholars!

IV- **Some, however, like the Psalmist, read the Bible joyfully.** It is their meat and drink. In it they hear God speak, and their fellowship with God is enlightened and deepened.

The wise Christian reads the Bible to commune with God. He reads it to learn of Jesus. The Scriptures, Jesus once said, "testify of me" (John 5:39). They should be read to keep life genuinely Christian.

According to this psalm, a right use of the Word does three things.

First, it keeps life clean. The man who delights in the teaching of God will avoid "the counsel of the ungodly," "the way of sinners," and "the seat of the scornful" (v. 1).

Second, it makes life fruitful. The Word-soaked man is like a well-watered tree, producing a good harvest of fruit.

18

"And he shall be like a tree planted by the rivers of water, that brings forth his fruit in his season" (v. 3). The Christian who really believes and practices the Bible will become increasingly Christlike. "The fruit of the Spirit," which is "love" (Gal. 5:22), will be produced in ever-increasing measure in his life.

Third, it prepares life for judgment. The righteous man will stand when the ungodly falls, "for the Lord knows the way of the righteous: but the way of the ungodly shall perish" (v. 6).

Read the Word of God. Do not read it as a religious charm, nor as a dreary duty. Do not read it in a negative spirit. Read it to hear God speak to your heart. Read it to get acquainted with Jesus Christ. Read it to give purpose and power to life. Read it to be holy, happy, and helpful. When you do, the reading of the Bible will become a delight to your soul. Speaking of impressions gained in childhood, Peter Townsend said, "I felt that I could trust the Bible; and ever since then I have felt that until you have got its message you have no inkling, whoever you are, of what life is really about." Happy the child or grown-up who has come to realize that truth.

O God, we would pray with the Psalmist, "Open my eyes that I may behold wondrous things out of your law."* Help us to read, study, digest, and practice Your Word, in order that our lives may be joyful, fruitful, and useful. Amen.

*Ps. 119:18

A Great Prayer

There are many great prayers in the Bible. They cover a vast range of human desires and needs. They respond to a great variety of precious promises from God. We are going to look at one of these prayers today. It is found in Psalm 19. Read slowly and thoughtfully through the entire psalm. How fitting are the words of verse 14. For those who want to please the Lord in their daily lives, there is not a more important prayer than the one found therein.

> *Let the words of my mouth, and the meditation of my heart, be acceptable in your sight, O Lord, my strength, and my redeemer.*

That would be a wise prayer to pray every day and even several times a day. More people have lost their religion by letting it run off their tongues than any other way. As James recognized, it would take a perfect man to bridle his tongue.

Notice the **sequence** in this prayer: "The words of my mouth and the meditation of my heart." The Psalmist was wise enough to know that the mouth is connected with the heart. What a person says will be determined by what he thinks. "As a man thinks in his heart, so is he" (Prov. 23:7). *If the heart is clean, the speech will be clean. If the heart is corrupt, the speech will be impure.* If the heart muses on God, the mouth will speak of God. If the heart muses on evil, the mouth will speak of evil. What comes out of the mouth depends upon what is stored in the heart.

That truth makes our reading habits very important. Read trash and you will talk trash. It may be best-seller trash, because good literature isn't determined by popularity. Nothing confirms the adage "A fool and his money are soon parted" like most best-selling novels. Fill your heart with truth and beauty. Read the Bible and the best of other books.

Yes, the mouth is connected to the heart. Your words are governed by your thoughts. There is no use praying for acceptable talking unless we pray for acceptable thinking.

II - *That brings us to the* **standard** *in this prayer.* Acceptable to whom? To the Lord: "acceptable in your sight, O Lord." Our thinking and talking are to please the Lord, not merely ourselves or others.

If people set the standard, it will be set too low. Today, books are filled with dirty words, movies are crammed with filthy scenes. Television programs are getting freer and freer with profanity and obscenity and blasphemy. Most speakers can't get through a speech without tossing in some smutty joke to entertain the crowd. Our society has a low standard of thought and speech. Some mothers used to wash their children's mouths out with soap for using bad language. Proctor and Gamble would be pushed to make enough soap to handle the situation today! Most youngsters would spend a lot of time blowing bubbles!

But the Lord sets the standard high. In His sight nothing passes that smirches His name, slanders His character, or corrupts the minds and lives of His people. He demands thinking and talking on a noble level. Listen to these words of Jesus about the importance of our words: "I say unto you, that every idle word that men shall speak, they shall give account thereof in the day of judgment. For by your words you shall be justified, and by your words you shall be condemned" (Matt. 12:36-37).

III - Confronted by this lofty standard, how can we measure up? *That brings us to the* **strength** *mentioned in this prayer:* "O Lord, my strength, and my redeemer." If we are going to

21

please God, we will need His strength to overcome temptation and to shuck off the influence of the world. We see and hear so much filth in our daily world that it's like living in a sewer. Only the strength of God can keep one's mind and mouth holy in the midst of the braying of moral jackasses. But thank God, the power for goodness and truth is available to us. We can be in the world but not of the world, according to Jesus Christ.

But what if we should stumble? What if we fall below the standard? Well, the Lord is our "redeemer." If we repent, He will forgive. If we submit, He will cleanse. This very psalm extols the thought and speech of God. His Word is described as perfect, sure, right, pure, clean, true, and sweeter than honey. By this Word we are converted, made wise, enlightened, and warned. *When we turn to God's thought and speech we find the deliverance we need when our mouths and hearts are not right.*

"Let the words of my mouth, and the meditation of my heart, be acceptable in your sight, O Lord, my strength, and my redeemer."* Amen.
*Ps. 19:4

22

A Prayer for Pardon

Isn't it good to ease your bones down into a chair and open up the Bible for a few minutes? Your whole day will go better if you spend some time thinking upon a portion of God's Word. The Psalmist prayed, "Lead me in your truth, and teach me: for you are the God of my salvation; on you I do wait all the day." That's not a bad prayer for us, is it? The prayer is found in the 25th psalm (v. 5). Let's look at another prayer in verse 11 of that same psalm:

> *For your name's sake, O Lord, pardon my iniquity; for it is great.*

If anyone wants forgiveness from God, that is just the prayer to pray. And who doesn't need forgiveness? Don't you? Just think back over your life—a few steps down memory lane should convince you. If you don't think you need forgiveness, ask your wife and children, or the crew at work, or even old Rover there. They can remind you of some iniquity that needs attention. Back in verse 7 the Psalmist cries, "Remember not the sin of my youth." Most of us don't have to go that far back to find a reason to cry out for pardon.

I – Let's take a closer look at this prayer now. <u>Notice first **the dimension of sin.**</u> "Pardon my iniquity; for *it is great.*"

We don't know the specific situation to which the Psalmist refers. If David wrote this prayer, it could refer to some hideous sins—adultery, murder, hypocrisy, to name a few leading candidates. No matter. The point is, *all sin is great, for it offends a great God, causes great damage to life, and can only be atoned for by a great price,* the blood of Jesus Christ.

23

No one ever got saved recommending himself to God. As long as a person says, "I'm not so bad," and tries to pass off his sins as mere trifles, he hasn't looked squarely into the mirror—or he is lying about what he saw. When a man gets honest about his sins he will feel like Paul did, that he is the chief of sinners.

Until you see your sins as great, you have not really seen God nor the cross of Christ nor your own defiled heart. When you do, however, sin will loom large enough to cast a shadow of misery over your entire life. But the shadow can be dispelled.

II – *That brings us to the* **ground of hope.** "For *your name's sake,* O Lord, pardon my iniquity."

The only reason God has for pardoning us is found within himself. We are totally without merit. That's true, neighbor, whatever your name is and whoever you think you are. You may be listed in Dun and Bradstreet and have your achievements catalogued in *Who's Who,* but *God cannot find any good reason to pardon you when He reads the name on your letterhead or mailbox.*

That goes for your ancestors, too. Some folks think they have a claim on God because they come from a line of blue bloods. Friend, you descend from a long line of sinners stretching back to Adam. If you knew the whole truth about your ancestors, you would quit bragging on your roots. You might go to the courthouse and have your name changed!

The sinner's only hope is given right here in verse 6: "Remember, O Lord, your tender mercies and your lovingkindnesses." Except for the love, mercy, and kindness of God, we would all be in hell before breakfast, and none of us would get out for supper.

"I put my trust in you," the Psalmist says to God. Not in myself, not in my coat of arms, not in my career achievements, only in God.

When God delivered ancient Israel from Egyptian bondage, it was for His own name's sake. When Moses pled with God to spare His ungrateful and disobedient people, he based his plea upon the name of God, not upon the merits of Israel. What was true of them is also true of us. We deserve judgment and wrath. *We are saved from our sins only because God cares too deeply for His people to let them perish without hope.*

Well, there you are. There is only one way out of sin, and that's by divine pardon. And pardon means a humbled man and a loving God. Climb down from the high horse of pride, confess your sin as great, and throw yourself on the mercy of God. His mercy bears the name of Jesus Christ, the Christ who said, "Come unto me, all you who labour and are heavy laden, and I will give you rest" (Matt. 11:28). Your own efforts to save yourself can never bring rest. Rest is found when we trust in Jesus Christ.

O Lord, like the Psalmist we pray, "Remember me for your goodness' sake," not for our goodness' sake. We deserve Your wrath. We plead for Your mercy. We have sinned, but Jesus died for our sins. He is our only hope. Save us, then, for Jesus' sake. Amen.

Two Invitations

Take a few minutes from your crowded schedule to read Psalm 66. Look at verse 5. It begins with the words

Come and see . . .

Now look at verse 16. This verse begins

Come and hear . . .

Two invitations are given. That is more than some of us get in a month. "Come and see . . . Come and hear . . ."

Come and see what? The verse goes on to say, "Come and see the works of God." *Come and see what God is doing.* Too many people cannot say that because God isn't doing anything in their lives. And too many churches cannot say that, either, for God isn't doing anything in their services. They are like the synagogue at Nazareth where Jesus could do no "mighty works . . . because of their unbelief" (Matt. 13:58; see Mark 6:5-6). *If you expect nothing from God, that is what you get,* and you get plenty of it.

What is God doing that is worth getting excited about? The Psalmist is talking about the Exodus: "He turned the sea into dry land: they went through the flood on foot" (v. 6). God's saving work, that is something to see! God opened the sea and a gang of Jewish slaves escaped from a pursuing Egyptian army.

When God is saving people, there is something to see. Lives are changed. People quit their meanness and start living right. They become free and happy, and it can be seen.

God's saving work is always visible. The bloody Cross could be seen. The empty tomb could be seen. The change in

26

the disciples could be seen. As Paul said to Festus and Agrippa "This thing was not done in a corner" (Acts 26:26). God delivers His knockout blows in the middle of the ring. God's saving work is up front and out loud. You know when it is happening.

II—Come and hear what? The Psalmist says, "I will declare what he has done for my soul." You *see the works of God,* and then you *hear the words of the saints.*

The order of these invitations is important and irreversible. If God is not doing anything, the church has nothing to talk about. When God is working, the church must bear witness to it. The apostles were told to put a lid on their preaching and they answered, "We cannot but speak the things which we have seen and heard" (Acts 4:20). Until God works there is nothing to talk about, but when God works there is no way to be quiet!

Look again at the Psalmist's testimony and notice how very personal it is: "what he has done for *my* soul." No matter how many slaves got out of Egypt, the question is, did *you* find freedom? No matter how many sinners are saved, the question is, did *you* get saved? Secondhand religion is not worth paying pew rent on, neighbor. Hearsay testimony is nothing more than religious gossip. Are *your* sins pardoned? Is *your* heart right with God?

If God is not working in your life or in your church, there is a good reason, and it's just as plain as the "amount owed" on a gas bill. Read verse 18: "If I regard iniquity in my heart, the Lord will not hear me." *God works in response to prayer.* You can pray like the priests of Baal on Mount Carmel, until you are bloody and bushed from the effort, but *if you will not break with sin God turns a deaf ear to your prayers.*

"Come and see." Can you say that? Is God working any miracles in your life, in your church? Are any waters being parted, any slaves of sin escaping into freedom? Or is it just ho hum—the same old stuff every Sunday?

"Come and hear." Can you say that? Have you got a personal experience and a personal testimony? It is a great thing to say, "The God of our fathers," but it does not amount to a hill of beans unless you can also say, "My God."

If you cannot issue these two invitations, are you willing to face up to the reason? The prophet Isaiah fingered that reason for ancient Israel—and for us—in these challenging words: "Behold, the Lord's hand is not shortened, that it cannot save; neither his ear heavy, that it cannot hear: but your iniquities have separated between you and your God, and your sins have hid his face from you, that he will not hear" (Isa. 59:1-2). If we forsake our sins and trust in His mercy, the Lord will act in our lives and churches as the God who does great things.

This wonderful psalm begins, "Make a joyful noise unto God . . . sing forth the honour of his name." That sounds like a celebration, doesn't it? That is what real Christianity is, a celebration! Is anything exciting happening to you? Do you have any reason to send out invitations?

O God, for Jesus' sake, work in our lives and in our churches until we have plenty of reason for joyful noises and confident invitations. Amen.

Thinking About God

Friend, I know you are busy. The days are crowded. Life is getting by fast. But you need to slow down a while and put your mind on what matters most. Pull up a chair, open up the Bible, and let God speak to your heart. Read Psalm 104. This is a great psalm extolling God as the majestic Creator. Let's focus our attention on verse 34:

My meditation of him shall be sweet: I will be glad in the Lord.

Everywhere the Psalmist looked he thought of God. He says in verse 24: "O Lord, how manifold are your works! in wisdom have you made them all: the earth is full of your riches." Some men go over the world with microscopes and telescopes and see nothing but blind chance and random force. They have Ph.D. brains and pygmy souls. The Psalmist thought of God as he looked upon nature. And every thought of God was pleasant, inspiring praise: "My meditation of him shall be sweet: I will be glad in the Lord."

That prompts a question: How do you feel when you think about God? Is it sweet, is it pleasant, or is it unpleasant and terrifying?

1 — How do you feel when you think of God? That depends upon your **conception** of Him.

Some religions have pictured God as cold, aloof, and uncaring about human life and destiny. According to one religious tradition, God took a chunk of clay in His hands, which represented the human race He would create, and broke it in two. He flung one part into heaven, saying, "These

29

to paradise, and I care not." He flung the other part into hell, saying, "These to hell, and I care not." No wonder the slogan arose, "Bring them to Islam by the sword."

Neighbor, the God of the Bible cares, cares so much that He gave His only Son to die for our salvation. He sought to barricade the road to hell with the broken body and shed blood of His dearest and best. When we conceive of God as the Father of our Lord Jesus Christ who loves us and sacrificed himself for us, then the thought of God humbles our minds and fills our hearts with praise.

_II_ _How do you feel when you think about God? That depends upon your_ **relation** _to Him._

It's not sweet to think about God _when you are sinning against Him._ The rebel doesn't enjoy the thought of his enemy. The criminal doesn't enjoy the thought of his judge. And when we trample God's love and laws, we try to keep too immersed in sin to think about the One who is perfectly holy and just.

Jacob sinned against Esau, and when he heard that Esau was riding to meet him with a posse, Jacob's conscience filled him with terror. He had to pray all night and get fixed up with God before he found courage to face his brother. Just so, if we are sinning against God, there is no comfort in the thought of meeting Him in judgment.

It's not sweet to think about God when you are _dying without Him._ Falstaff, the sinner, as he was dying, cried out, "God! God! God!" And the woman who was attending him said, "I to comfort him bids him that he should not think of God." Neighbor, I don't want to live in such a way that my dying comfort depends on crowding God from my thoughts.

What a contrast to this was John Wesley's passing. Worn out from serving God, he met death saying, "Best of all, God is with us." When you live for God you can die in peace, and the thought of God will be your deepest joy.

This psalm begins, "Bless the Lord, O my soul. O Lord my God, you are very great." And it closes with the words, "Praise the Lord." When you can say, "*My* God," it will be sweet to think about Him. Secondhand religion couldn't bless a frog enough to make him croak, much less a man enough to make him sing. But warm, intimate, personal communion with God will make you "sing unto the Lord."

Samuel Rutherford, a brave Scottish Covenanter, was flung into prison for his faith in Christ. In his journal we find an entry which reads, "Jesus Christ came into my cell last night, and every stone in the wall flashed like a ruby." The presence of the Lord was radiant and precious to a man who loved, trusted, and served Him. Such blessed communion with God is possible for us all.

O Lord, Creator of all that is, and Savior of all who believe, we confess You with joy. You are our Maker and Redeemer, and every thought of You is honey in our hearts. Receive our praise and thanks for being such a God and saving such a people. In Jesus' name. Amen.

A Life-changing Vision

Isaiah 6 is one of the great sections of the Old Testament. The high-water mark of ancient Israel's understanding of God is found in the writings of Isaiah. And the vision recorded in this chapter shaped his thinking and preaching. Here is the source and mold of his theology. Read the first three verses:

> In the year that king Uzziah died I saw also the Lord sitting upon a throne, high and lifted up, and his train filled the temple. Above it stood the seraphims . . . And one cried unto another, and said, Holy, holy, holy, is the Lord of hosts: the whole earth is full of his glory.

The king was dead and the prophet grieved. He had pinned his hopes on the earthly monarch. God decided to show Isaiah who really was king of Israel—and over the whole earth. So He revealed himself to the prophet, a God exalted in holiness and power.

The effect of that vision is caught up in three little words: "Woe," "lo," and "go."

I—The prophet said, "Woe," the word of conviction. "Woe is me! for I am undone; because I am a man of unclean lips, and I dwell in the midst of a people of unclean lips: for mine eyes have seen the King, the Lord of hosts" (v. 5). The dazzling holiness of God made the prophet aware of, and ashamed of, his own unholiness. He was struck dumb. He could not join the anthem of the seraphim who were ascribing holiness to God. He waited to be slain by the awesome power of that divine holiness.

32

Mark it down, neighbor, the man who doesn't know himself as an unclean sinner has never seen the Lord. Stack your life against the life of Jesus, the Son of God, and you will cry out as Simon Peter did, "Depart from me; for I am a sinful man, O Lord" (Luke 5:8).

II—**The seraphim said, "Lo," the word of cleansing.** "Lo, this has touched your lips; and your iniquity is taken away, and your sin purged."

God doesn't want to destroy sinners, He wants to destroy sin. The live coal from the altar—what a beautiful symbol of the cleansing of our hearts through the blood of Jesus and by the power of the Holy Spirit! That is God's answer to man's cry of conviction.

Sin is deep-rooted and longstanding. The lips are unclean because the heart is impure, for "out of the abundance of the heart the mouth speaks" (Matt. 12:34). God provides, through the altar and the fire, an inward and outward holiness that means life instead of death. No man has to live with garbage in his heart and trash on his lips. "The blood of Jesus Christ his Son cleanses us from all sin" (1 John 1:7). We can get the poison of sin out of our hearts and stop spreading it to others with our mouths. We can be forgiven, renewed, and cleansed!

III—**God said, "Go," the word of commission.** "And he said, Go, and tell this people . . ." (v. 9).

As soon as his sin was purged Isaiah heard "the voice of the Lord" calling for message bearers to his people: "Whom shall I send, and who will go for us?" (v. 8). Isn't it marvelous how grace improves hearing! The prophet volunteered on the spot without raising a question about salary, fringe benefits, or retirement plan. Neighbor, the unclean heart thinks of itself, just as unclean lips speak for themselves. Sin is self-centeredness. But the cleansed heart cares for others and the purged lips speak for God. True holiness is oriented toward God and society.

God said, "Go," but warned Isaiah that few would listen. The results of his ministry would be like the charred stump of a felled tree. He would have little to show for his efforts. No wonder the prophet cried, "Lord, how long?" Notice God's reply: "Until the cities be wasted without inhabitant" (v. 11). As long as there are people who need to hear, you are to go on speaking. *We don't serve because we are wanted but because we are needed*. We don't take God's Word to others because we are assured of success. We do it because He says, "Go and tell," and that leaves us no option. The holy heart is obedient and durable. It salutes like an army sergeant and endures like an army mule!

Isaiah saw God, saw himself, and saw a needy world. The visions hang together and follow one another in logical sequence. Saving grace comes from God, touches our lives with power, and reaches out through us to embrace others. Is the prophet's experience your experience, too? You may not see the vision as he did, but you can know the cleansing and share the calling to bear witness. The trappings of the vision are incidental. The experience of grace is essential.

O Lord of hosts, You are thrice holy, and we are just that unholy until Your fire purges our hearts. May Your Holy Spirit apply the blood of Jesus Christ to our hearts, that our lips may tell others of Your grace and goodness. Do it now, Lord! Amen.

Repentance

Fetch your Bible and read Matt. 3:1-10. Here is recorded, in part, the ministry of John the Baptist. He was a strange figure, recalling the past (the golden age of Israel's prophets) and announcing the future (the glorious age of Israel's Messiah). John launched his fearless, fruitful ministry with these words, in verse 2:

Repent: for the kingdom of heaven is at hand.

When Jesus began to preach, He took up the same message: "Repent, for the kingdom of heaven is at hand" (4:17). When the apostles went forth to preach the gospel to all nations, they echoed the same demanding, promising truth: "Repent, and be converted, that your sins may be blotted out" (Acts 3:19). Today the message of repentance is needed as much as ever before. Sin is still offensive to God. Sinners are still under His judgment. The words of our Lord are still true: "Unless you repent, you shall . . . perish" (Luke 13:3, 5).

1—This account of John's ministry sets before us **the need** for repentance. "Repent, for the kingdom of heaven is at hand." Unless we repent of our sins, we cannot enter the kingdom of heaven. Jesus Christ came as God's anointed King, to rule over all who will become God's redeemed people. *He is heaven's King, and His rule over our hearts and lives is heaven's kingdom.*

What is called "the kingdom of heaven" in Matthew is called "the kingdom of God" in the other Gospels. The same fact is elsewhere referred to as "salvation" and "eternal life." This kingdom has no geographical boundaries, no specific

35

political forms. It does not consist of externals such as creeds or rituals or polity. "The kingdom of God," said Paul, "is not meat and drink; but righteousness, and peace, and joy in the Holy Spirit. For he that in these things serves Christ is acceptable to God, and approved of men" (Rom. 14:17-18). To be in the kingdom of God is to serve Jesus Christ in righteousness, peace, and joy.

Salvation is an exchange of kingdoms. As Paul described it, "God has delivered us from the power of darkness, and has transferred us into the kingdom of his dear Son" (Col. 1:13). *Every person is ruled either by sin or by God. To be ruled by sin is death; to be ruled by God is life.* If you wish to pass from death to life, from sin to God, you must repent.

II. *John has something to teach us also about* **the evidence** *of repentance.* Certain religious leaders wanted John to baptize them. They wanted to jump on the bandwagon of a movement growing in popularity. John refused, saying, "O generation of vipers, who has warned you to flee from the wrath to come? Bring forth therefore fruits that evidence repentance" (Matt. 3:7-8).

One evidence of repentance is confession of sins. Those who believed John's preaching were "baptized by him in Jordan, confessing their sins" (v. 6).

But confession is not enough. Sin must be forsaken. The life-style must be changed. Some confess their sins with no intention of leaving their sins. They want to be saved *in* their sins, not *from* their sins. *God will not make a deal with sin. You either quit your sins or kiss your hope of salvation good-bye.*

Luke's Gospel tells how various groups of people came to John the Baptist asking, "What shall we do?" John told them to start living honestly, peacefully, and unselfishly. John's brand of repentance did not allow for any willful continuance of sin.

Unless you break clean and clear from sin, God will not pardon your sins and welcome you to His kingdom.

III • Is the price too high? Is the demand too rigid? Multitudes have heard the gospel and refused the Kingdom; they did not want to give up their sins. *Anyone tempted to reject Christ should consider **the alternative** to repentance.*

"Who has warned you to flee from the wrath to come?" (v. 7).

God's holy wrath is coming upon sin. God will bring an awful final judgment upon evildoers. Jesus said, "Unless you repent, you shall . . . perish." To perish is to die eternally, to be separated from God forever. Existence will never be filled with meaning, or with peace, or with joy. The deep inward hungers of the soul will go forever unsatisfied. The torment of alienation from God, of the loss of true identity and true humanity, will be endless! *When God calls you to repentance, the issue is heaven or hell!*

"Repent, for the kingdom of heaven is at hand!"

O God, who will be our Judge, who would be our Savior, help us to repent honestly, to believe simply, and to rejoice eternally. In Christ's name. Amen.

Not by Bread Alone

How quickly can you find your Bible? Is it under a pile of newspapers? Is it in a cluttered desk drawer? Americans should keep their Bibles near the television schedule, then they would see them every day!

Open your Bible to Matthew's Gospel, chapter 4. Here is recorded the temptation of Christ in the wilderness. Verses 3 and 4 tell us:

> When the tempter came to him, he said, If you are the son of God, command that these stones be made bread. But he answered and said, It is written, Man shall not live by bread alone, but by every Word that proceeds out of the mouth of God.

Let me ask you a question. How long has it been since you had some bread? Unless you are sick, you had some within the past few hours. If you were lucky it was corn bread, with some collard greens and fried chicken to go along with it. Now that will help a fellow pour cement or plow corn!

Well, how long has it been since you had a square meal of Bible reading and study? Think hard. Can you remember? That's why some people who are 40 pounds overweight physically can't cast a shadow spiritually.

Man needs bread, but he needs the Bible even more.

I- **Without the Bible you can't find God.** God has revealed himelf in Christ, and the Bible is the only history of that divine self-disclosure.

II—**Without the Bible you don't know how to live.** The purpose of life for a creature is to do the Creator's will. God's will is declared to us only in the Bible.

III **Without the Bible you don't have any power against the devil.** The only defense against the subtlety and power of the tempter is that one exercised by Jesus Christ—"It is written."

In this section of Matthew's Gospel, you can see that the devil was clawing at Jesus tooth and nail; he was trying to get Jesus to doubt the Father's love, to presume upon the Father's care, and to substitute for the Father's will. Jesus defeated the devil and kept His relationship to God unspoiled because He knew the Bible and lived by it. Every time the devil stuck his head up and spouted a temptation, Jesus clobbered him by replying, "It is written . . ."

Jesus never wrote a book, but He certainly knew what was written in God's Book! Lots of people are writing books about religion who don't know what God has written. Jesus did, and we had better if we want to be saved and to live for God.

Out of the mouth of God proceed words! God talks, and unlike a lot of preachers and politicians, when God talks He says something. He speaks words for living—for living as His child, for living by His plans. God's words are holy, and His words give us power for following Jesus and for fighting evil.

Of course, *the Bible must be lived, not just read.* Some folks read it, dissect it, and argue about it who don't put it into shoe leather. It has to be lived, not just read. But you can't live it until you do read it and know what it teaches.

Another thing: Jesus says that we are to live by *every* word that proceeds from God's mouth. You can't go to the Bible like you do to a cafeteria, and say, I'll take this but not that. I'll obey this but not that. I'll believe what it says about

39

love, but not what it says about wrath. I'll cling to its promises, but I'll ignore its demands.

When the devil jumped on Jesus the second time, the devil himself quoted scripture. Think of it—the devil with a Bible in his hand sounding like a preacher! But he yanked that quotation out of context and misapplied it. Taking parts of the Bible and using them for our own advantage is devilish.

Friend, the devil is after you. You may not be such big game to him as was Jesus, but he wants to destroy your life. And if you don't want him to succeed, you must get busy with that Bible. *Read it. Believe it. Practice it.*

John Wesley said, "I want to know one thing—the way to heaven; how to land safe on that happy shore. God Himself has condescended to teach the way; for this very end He came from heaven. He hath written it down in a book. O give me that Book! At any price, give me the book of God! I have it: here is knowledge enough for me. Let me be *homo unius liber.* Here then I am, far from the busy ways of men. I sit down alone: only God is here. In His presence I open, I read His book; for this end, to find the way to heaven."

Yes, God has written in a book the way to life and heaven. The next time you shake hands with a knife and fork in front of a plate of hot biscuits and honey, just remember: "Man shall not live by bread alone, but by every word that proceeds out of the mouth of God."

O God, give us hearty appetites for Your Word, and help us to feed on it daily for strength, so that we can please You, defeat the devil, and count for the Kingdom. In Jesus' name. Amen.

Sinker and Saver

I hope you are having a good day so far. If you are, you can make it better with time out for the Bible. And if you are not, that is even more reason to put your cares aside and pick your Bible up.

Turn to Matt. 14:22-33. Think especially on these words in verses 30 and 31:

> *But when he saw the wind boisterous, he was afraid; and beginning to sink, he cried, saying, Lord, save me. And immediately Jesus stretched forth his hand, and caught him, and said unto him, O you of little faith, wherefore did you doubt?*

Peter tried to walk on the water to Jesus, but the wind was strong and the waves were high, and he was about to go glug, glug, glug! He did not step out of that boat as a man of faith anyhow. Look at verse 28: Peter said, "Lord, if it is you, bid me come unto you on the water." If! Who else would it have been but Jesus? Who else cared that "the wind was contrary" and those disciples were in danger? Who else would come to them through the storm "in the fourth watch of the night"? Of course it was Jesus! But Peter said, "If." *A man with "if" in his heart and no webs on his feet cannot walk on water!* Peter began to sink and he began to pray.

Praying was the only smart thing he did in this whole story. Some people are sinking but their pride keeps them from praying. During the depression some preachers wanted F. D. Roosevelt to call a national day of prayer. He said, "We got into this mess ourselves, and we will get out the same

41

way." That is a paraphrase, not a verbatim quote. Well, he was a Democrat, but right then he was as foolish as any Republican has ever been. Whatever your politics or religion, when you are sinking you should be praying. It is better to swallow your pride than to swallow the lake. *Praying beats drowning any day, including Monday.*

Look at Peter's prayer: "Lord, save me." *The higher the waves the shorter the prayers*—have you noticed that? Most of the honest prayers we make are cries for help. When things are rosy we tend to make flowery speeches to God. In the sinking times we just holler for help.

If you really mean business with God, short prayers are long enough. I am talking about prayers of petition. Prayers of thanksgiving take longer because we have so much to be thankful for. And prayers of communion take longer, for its such a joy to be in God's presence that prayer stretches out. But when you are sinking, when you need saving, the link between God and you is a short and simple cry for help.

It is not the length of prayer but the strength of prayer that counts, and the strength of prayer is sincerity. Jesus warned us not to pray to be seen of men but to be heard of God, and God hears and answers the sincere prayer.

That comment brings us to the answer. "And immediately Jesus stretched forth his hand, and caught him" (v. 31). Remember, neighbor, Jesus was the incarnate Word of God. He came to show us what God is like. "He that has seen me has seen the Father," Jesus said (John 14:9). *What a picture of God—God with His hand outstretched to save us!*

Saving people is Jesus' business. "The Son of man is come to seek and to save that which was lost" (Luke 19:10). Saving is His business, and He is good at His business! *There is no one in the world that God does not love and that Jesus cannot save.* The writer of Hebrews hit the bull's-eye when he said, "He is able to save them to the uttermost that come unto God by him" (7:25).

42

Jesus escorted His dripping disciple back to the boat and climbed aboard. The men in the boat "worshipped him, saying, Of a truth you are the Son of God" (v. 33). The Son of God is the Savior of all who will cry to Him for help. We cannot save ourselves. The other folks in the boat cannot save us. Only Jesus can save us. But Jesus is not a last resort, He is the first with the most!

Are you sinking in your sins? Are the waters of sickness or trouble or grief or pain washing over your head? Are you helpless in the boisterous wind of adversity or bereavement? Are you drowning in loneliness or guilt or fear? Whatever the waves that menace your life today, Jesus can save you. Let your sinking times become praying times. Briefly and honestly call upon the Lord for deliverance. Trust yourself to His love and power. You will discover that He is the God of the outstretched hand and mighty arm!

O Lord, the waves are high, the boat is small, and we are sinking. Come to us. Reach out Your hand and save us. Where we know sin, guilt, and fear, let us have forgiveness, peace, and joy. Get us safely to the far shore where we will be at home with You forever! Amen.

Pilate's Question
—Your Answer

Read chapter 27 of Matthew's Gospel. Here is the record of Jesus' trial before the Roman governor, Pontius Pilate. Have you been on trial, neighbor? Have you been before a judge? Well, you will be some day! "We shall all stand before the judgment seat of Christ" (Rom. 14:10). That's why Pilate's question is the most important question ever asked. Read it there in verse 22:

> *Pilate said unto them, What shall I do then with Jesus which is called Christ?*

Called Christ, my eye! He *is* Christ, the One anointed by God to be the Savior of sinners. His claim, however, was rejected. He was called other things—glutton, drunkard, lawbreaker, demon-collaborator, to name a few of them. His name-calling enemies hounded Him to His death on the Cross, calling Him blasphemer. But God raised Him from the dead, saying by that mighty act, "Jesus is both Lord and Christ."

Pilate's question is your question. Jesus is before you as surely as He was before Pilate. Because He is Lord and Savior, because He will be Judge, you cannot evade Him. Trying to escape this question is like trying to escape your shadow. You plunge into the dark, wipe your brow, and say, It's gone. But as soon as light hits you, there it is again. You can wade into sin up to your eyes and think you're rid of Jesus. But in your sober moods and honest moments, there He is again, saying, "What are you going to do with Me?"

II. **Pilate's dilemma is your dilemma.** He had to do something with Jesus, and so do you. There was no way to be neutral, no way to avoid decision. Pilate's hand-washing act fooled nobody. His disclaimer of guilt was a farce. He said, "I am innocent of the blood of this just person" (v. 24), but he was as guilty as the devil and he knew it.

Pilate's wife said, "Have nothing to do with that just man" (v. 19). Like much of the advice a man gets from his wife, it wasn't worth the breath it took to give it. Jesus was on Pilate's hands. He had to do something. And the gospel message leaves you with no third alternative. There's no way to say, "I'll just ignore the matter." That in itself is a decision, and a wicked, insane decision at that.

Poor Pilate was pulled apart by his conscience and his fear. He wanted to release Jesus, but he was afraid the Jews would start a ruckus. And he was afraid of Caesar, for his boss took a dim view of weak governors who allowed revolts to occur in the provinces. Pilate was like Paul Barnes' one-eyed cat, worn out from trying to watch two ratholes at the same time. What are you afraid of if you say yes to Jesus?

III. **Pilate's answer need not be your answer.** Pilate rejected Jesus. He lined up with the Christ-hating, Christ-crucifying mob. He caved in to popular opinion. He lacked the courage to do what he knew was right and take the consequences. "He delivered Jesus to be crucified" (v. 26).

Christ is not an escape from trouble, only an escape from sin. If you go with Christ you'll be on a collision course with the world, the flesh, and the devil—with a few of your kinfolks thrown in for bad measure. But if you reject Christ, hoping to save your hide, you'll lose your soul. *Better to be abused by men than condemned by God.* As Jesus put it, "Fear not them which kill the body, but are not able to kill the soul;

45

but rather fear him which is able to destroy both soul and body in hell" (Matt. 10:28).

In Jesus Christ you gain more than you lose. The most you can lose is your life, and thousands of martyrs have. But you gain the forgiveness of sins, peace with God, freedom to be your true self, a share in the greatest work of all time, and everlasting life besides. Pilate struck a fool's bargain. You don't have to repeat it.

Let's lay it on the line. "What shall I do with Jesus?" You must do something. You have but two choices—reject Him or accept Him. Reject Him and all is lost in hell. Accept Him and all is gained in heaven. Make up your mind—it's the most urgent question you will ever answer.

A man was dying in great pain but with great peace. Friends marveled at his calmness in the midst of anguish. He said, "Over 40 years ago I said yes to Jesus. He delivered me from the living hell of alcoholism. I just formed the habit of saying yes to Him, and He has kept me in peace through every trial." You can live and die at peace with God by saying yes to Christ.

Almighty God, You can destroy body and soul in hell. And that's what we all deserve for our sins. But You gave Your Son for us, to become our Savior and Lord. Help us to say yes to Him and take the consequences. In His name we pray. Amen.

"And Certain Women"

Open your Bible to Luke's Gospel, chapter 8. We are going to take a look at the women in Jesus' life. If I had used any name but Jesus, you might have expected some gossip. But Jesus is the one Man who never sinned against God or with others. He was slandered, but only liars and knaves had anything bad to say about Him. And that is just as true today as it was back in century one.

Look at the closing words of verse 1, the opening words of verse 2, and the closing words of verse 3. Did that confuse you? Actually, you can see all three verses at once, so it will get clear as we read.

The twelve were with him, and certain women ...
which ministered unto him of their substance.

The 12 disciples were with Jesus, but the Twelve were not enough. As hard as they tried, as much as they did, the men who walked and worked with Jesus were not enough. The ministry of these precious women was vital to the mission of Christ.

Is this not true today? *Take the women out of the church, and it would fail in two weeks' time.* They have worked harder, prayed more, and cooperated better than the men have throughout the church's history. And most of the time they have done it while taking a lot of guff from the men.

A few of these women are named, most of them are unnamed, but all of them are important. Mary, Joanna, and Susanna are named. They were prominent for whatever reasons. With them were "many others"—lumped together in the record without being named. But it was the sum total of what they did that made the work of Jesus possible.

Things don't change much, do they? A few folks in the church are center stage with the light on them. Their names are well known and often called. But the great host of God's workmen and workwomen give their service quietly—no bugles blowing, no flags waving, no cameras clicking, no reporters writing. They do it because they love Jesus, not because they want publicity. But if they didn't serve, the old ship of Zion would sink faster than a torpedoed banana boat.

Who they were is not important; what they did was: They ministered to Jesus.

I - Some of them provided money. That's what Scripture means when it says, "of their substance." They shelled out money for the support of this Preacher-Teacher-Healer named Jesus, who was helping and saving hundreds of people wherever He went.

God's work always needs money, and He doesn't send it down from heaven. People supply it from grateful hearts and consecrated purses. And no group has a better record for sacrificial giving than the women who serve Jesus. Like the widow who gave all she had—you can read about her in chapter 21—many women have been willing to invest their last dollar in the work of the Kingdom, while rich men give paltry sums that wouldn't make a decent tip in a third-class restaurant.

II - Other women provided service. They cooked and served the meals, and they probably laundered the clothes. If Jesus had been forced to eat meals cooked by the Twelve, He might have died from ulcers before He could reach the Cross to die for our sins.

The role of women isn't stereotyped in the New Testament. Not all women cooked and cleaned. There were businesswomen and even women preachers. We thank God, nevertheless, for those who catered the meals for the Son of God!

III. **Still other women provided testimony.** When Jesus preached the gospel they furnished living evidence of its power to transform human life. They had been "healed of evil spirits and infirmities" (v. 2). They were walking advertisements of what the love and power of Jesus could do for sinners. The most dramatic case among them was Mary Magdalene, "out of whom went seven devils" when Jesus said, "Scat!"

The gospel needs preachers to spread it abroad, but it needs witnesses to make it convincing. There is no higher service to God than the witness of a life renewed by His grace.

Look around you, friend, and you will see godly women who quietly serve Jesus Christ. Their lives are outpourings of love to Him and service to others. They pray and give and worship and witness, making every sacrifice possible to extend the mission of the Master in this lost, broken world. Their lives make a cynic's contempt for religion false, cheap, and self-serving. Such women are the ultimate arguments for the reality of Christ's saving power.

Lord, we thank You for the good women who helped You then and who help You now. Bless their lives and their work, and keep them from a scheming devil and from corrupt men. Amen.

When the Devil Drives

Our Bible break today is also in Luke 8. While you're looking it up, offer a prayer of thanksgiving to God for your Bible. It costs far less than your easy chair, golf clubs, or TV set, but it's your most valuable possession. It tells you how to find God and get to heaven, and no other book does that.

In Luke 8 there is a quaint story told in verses 26-39. A demon-possessed man, a maniac, confronted Jesus and discovered one man who was not afraid of him. Furthermore, Jesus didn't want to cage him up, He wanted to set him free. So He cast out the demons, after giving them permission to enter a herd of swine feeding on the hillside. Now read again verse 33:

> Then went the devils out of the man, and entered into the swine: and the herd ran violently down a steep place into the lake, and were choked.

Those stampeding hogs are a dramatic illustration of what happens when human life is controlled by demonic forces, of what happens when the devil drives.

I. **When the devil drives, the direction is down.** "The herd ran violently down . . ."

A man in sin is better today than he will be tomorrow. It is the nature of sin to drag a person down, down, down. Sin's center of gravity is hell, and every godless life is tending in that direction.

From a "harmless" social drink many a man or woman has gone down and hit the bottom of a drunkard's empty life. From a little poker for pennies, many a man has become

50

addicted to gambling, going down until he ends up losing job, family, everything. Nobody ever starts playing with fire intending to burn himself. No one ever took a first step in sin expecting to go all the way to its rat-infested basement. But that is how sin works when the devil drives. Things keep getting worse.

II - **When the devil drives, the speed is fast.** "The herd ran violently down . . ."

Nothing pleases the devil more than the frantic pace of modern life. He's a speed demon! Sometimes I think the devil's three favorite words are "Hurry, hurry, hurry." He doesn't want people to stop and think; he just wants them to keep rushing down to destruction.

The gospel invites reflection. God says, "Come now, and let us reason together" (Isa. 1:18). One of the common verbs for preaching in the Book of Acts is "reasoning." Remember Jesus' story of the prodigal son? He left his father, wasted his life, and ended up in a hog lot. In that hogpen the prodigal "came to himself" (Luke 15:17). He started thinking about his situation. Until then the trail was down. But when he reflected seriously on his life, then he said, "I will arise and go to my father" (v. 18). As long as the devil can keep us from thinking, he can keep us heading for hell like a bat for its dark cave.

III - **When the devil drives, the end is ruin.** "The herd ran violently down a steep place into the lake, and were choked."

Demons drove the hogs to suicide. And the evil forces which grip and drive human life always bring it to ruin. The world is full of people who were brought to *physical* ruin by their sins. All kinds of crippling and killing diseases are directly related to wicked living. Other thousands are brought down to *mental* ruin. Guilt, unrelieved by God's pardon, cracks up people and fills up asylums. And multitudes are being brought down to *eternal* ruin. The hogs' path ended in

51

a lake where they thrashed about and drowned. The way of sin leads down to "the lake of fire," a terrifying picture of the ultimate ruin caused by sin.

A friend of mine was being driven down. He was addicted to drugs, and his life had become empty and useless. In disgust and despair he deliberately drove his car over a beachside cliff. To his shock the car was caught and held by a tree growing out of the face of the cliff. Shaken by the aborted suicide attempt, he went to church, heard the gospel, and gave his heart to Christ. Today he is a preacher of the Word of God.

You don't have to be driven to ruin by the forces of evil. You can be saved from sin. There is just one answer to sin, and that is to turn life over to Jesus Christ. When He is your Savior and Lord, the trail leads upward and ends in heaven.

Where are you headed today?

O Jesus, evil forces are destroying human lives. People are going down fast to ruin. Stop them. Slow them down and make them think. Save them from sin and hell. No one else can, but You are able! Help them to put life in Your hands. And those of us who have found You, help us to keep life in Your hands. Amen.

Somebody!

Let's rest awhile and break bread together. I don't mean buttermilk biscuits; I mean the Word of the Lord. Open your Bible to the section we've been looking at, Luke 8. There is a question recorded in verse 45 that I want us to think about.

Jesus said, Who touched me?

Do you know the story? A little woman was slowly bleeding to death. The victim of an incurable hemorrhage, she had trudged from doctor to doctor seeking help. They could not cure her, but they took all her money. Mark says she suffered many things of many physicians. Luke, being a doctor and sympathetic to the profession, omits that detail.

Then this woman heard of Jesus, a strange healer who had helped so many people. So she slipped through the crowd, took the hem of His robe between her trembling fingers, and the bleeding stopped immediately. Jesus stopped, looked around, and asked, "Who touched me?" He knew that power had gone from Him to heal someone.

Now it isn't the question so much as the answers that we need to look at. Three answers were given. The first two were wrong. Jesus brushed them aside and supplied the right answer himself.

I— "Who touched me?" **The crowd said, "Nobody."** Luke's exact words are "all denied." The sad truth is, where that crowd was concerned the woman was nobody. She isn't named. She had no friends. She had no money. Everyone she sought help from had been unable to give it. Nameless, friendless, moneyless, and helpless—that is about as near nobody as you can be!

~II~ "Who touched me?" **The disciples said, "Everybody."** "Master," they said in exasperation, "the multitude throng you and press you." Jesus drew crowds quicker than a fire engine can, and everybody wanted to get close enough to see and to hear Him. There was a lot of shoving and elbowing and toe-stomping, and the disciples got tired of it.

Their answer was no better than the crowd's. If you are "everybody" you are still "nobody." If you are just a face in the crowd, a number in an account book, or a hole in an IBM card, you become depersonalized and dehumanized. Life is then emptied of value. You can be terribly lonesome in a crowd where no one knows who you are or cares how you are getting along.

"Who touched me?" **Jesus' answer was, "Somebody."** Look at verse 46: "Jesus said, Somebody has touched me: for I perceive that virtue is gone out of me." *Everybody is somebody to Jesus.* He cares for the poor, the sick, the hurt, the lost. He sees the individual in the crowd. That is a truth designed to elicit our praise!

The little woman came and confessed and testified. Then something beautiful happened. Jesus called her "Daughter." He adopted her without bothering to climb the courthouse steps. This was love at work and it could not wait for law. Talk about somebody, she was now the daughter of the King! Just how important can you get?

As the daughter of Jesus, this woman was given some marvelous presents—health and peace. Jesus said, "Daughter, be of good comfort: your faith has made you whole; go in peace" (v. 48). Think of it!

Talk about a Cinderella story! Talk about a rags to riches story! This woman went from nobody to somebody with no intermediate stops. She went from a dying unknown to the health-crowned, peace-filled daughter of the Lord himself!

And it all happened because she touched Jesus. *The crowds pressed Him, but she touched Him.* They were merely curious, she was desperate. They were spectators, she was involved. It is the hurting, helpless, hungry folks who touch Jesus in faith and get help. For all its thronging the crowd was unchanged, but this woman was healed, adopted, and saved!

Friend, you matter to Jesus. He sees you, cares for you, and makes His saving power available to you. You are not just one of the crowd, unknown, unloved, unwept. You are a person for whom Jesus died, a person to whom Jesus calls, saying, "Come unto me, . . . and I will give you rest" (Matt. 11:28). Yes, you matter to Jesus.

Do you matter to yourself? Are you going to let the unfeeling crowd define your worth? Are you going to drift on in your sin and guilt and lostness, doing nothing about it? This woman rejected the crowd's indifference. She made up her mind to get to Jesus and to touch Him in faith. If you will do that, like her you can become somebody, the somebody God made you to be. *Sin has unmade you, but Jesus can remake you.* He will save and adopt you as you trust in Him today.

Lord Jesus, we would touch You in faith. Don't let the crowds hold us back. The world tries to make us nobodies, and it almost succeeds. Make us somebodies by Your healing, pardoning, adopting love. Amen.

Women Made Straight

Are you having trouble with your wife? Or with your mother-in-law? Do you get angry and say, "Just wait till I get my hands on her"? Well, your hands will only make things worse. If a woman is doing wrong, what she needs is for Jesus Christ to get His hands on her.

Open your Bible to Luke 13. There, in verses 10 through 17, you have the story of a woman who was marvelously helped and changed by Jesus. Verse 13 reads:

> *And he laid his hands on her: and immediately she was made straight, and glorified God.*

Jesus can straighten out a woman. Isn't that something!

I — **He straightened out this woman physically.** Poor soul, she had a crippling ailment that kept her bowed down in a painful and grotesque manner. She had been unable to lift herself erect for 18 years, long, misery-filled years.

In spite of her suffering she was "in one of the synagogues on the sabbath." Go into any church on any Sunday and you will find women serving God more faithfully in sickness than most men do in health. They put the men to shame. And the sorriest man in the lot is the one who dismisses religion with contempt, saying, "That stuff is for the women and children." A fellow doesn't stay away from church because he is a man, but because he is a wicked rascal, as full of sin as a watermelon is of juice.

"Jesus saw her"—that's what verse 12 says. He would, you know, because He looked for people who needed help. He called her over and said, "Woman, you are loosed from

56

your infirmity." Then "he laid his hands on her" and she was immediately healed. She stood erect, joy shining on her face, gratitude bursting from her heart.

A jarring note is struck in verse 14. The "ruler of the synagogue" complained about the woman's healing. To him the healing was a violation of the Sabbath law against work. The woman didn't matter to him. Jesus accused him of thinking more of animals than of people. Lots of men are like that. Their wives would like to have the affection that their horses or hounds get! Notice that Jesus didn't call this objector a male chauvinist pig. He called him a hypocrite. That's a pig pretending to be a sheep.

II - *Jesus straightened this woman physically, but* **He straightened up some women mentally.** Mary Magdalene is an example. He cast seven demons out of her, and that's not the world record! I knew a woman who was emotionally ill and acted like a demon in her home. One of those healing preachers came through town, looked into her case, and said she had seven demons in her. I told him that his intentions were good but his count was low!

Mentally and emotionally, people are cracking up right and left. Modern life is a pressure cooker. *But the touch and teaching of Jesus can do more to straighten people out than all the mind doctors listed in the Yellow Pages.*

III - **Jesus straightened out other women morally.** They brought to Him a woman caught in the act of adultery. The men wanted to kill her—maybe to keep her from talking! Jesus said, "He that is without sin among you, let him first cast a stone at her" (John 8:7). That broke up the rock-throwing party in a hurry. Every man slunk away, whipped down the street by his own conscience. And Jesus said to the woman, "Go, and sin no more." He didn't condone adultery, but he saved the adulteress. *He doesn't justify ungodliness, but He does justify the ungodly.* His love and mercy lifted her eyes

57

to the possibility of a new life. She straightened up and went out to be a different woman.

What a Savior is Jesus! Wouldn't it be wonderful if He could put His hands on every crooked person in our community? And on every twisted thing in our lives? And on every warped notion in our religion? *He can straighten us all out if we will do what this woman did, come when He calls.*

Sex is no barrier to the saving power of Jesus. He can straighten up men as well as women, even though they usually manage to become more crooked than the women.

Time is no barrier to His saving power, either. Here He heals a woman who had been crooked for 18 years. On another occasion He healed a man who had been helpless for 38 years. Whether sin has bound you for 8 years or 80, Jesus is able to set you free. Let Him lay His holy, mighty hands upon your crooked life, and you can be straightened up to serve the Lord in newness of life.

I don't want to bob the tail of verse 13. It closes with the words "and glorified God." When people are touched and freed by Jesus, you are going to hear praises from their lips!

Lord, we praise You for Your power to straighten up the crooked and lift up the oppressed. Help us to attend church faithfully where that power is so often demonstrated. Put Your loving hands upon us all! Amen.

Short, Sought, Saved

Welcome again to the Word of God. The Bible is a hall of mirrors, a portrait gallery, a place to see yourself in others, to learn the truth about yourself from God.

Ah, the truth! How devastating to pride it can be. The truth strips sin of its hiding place. The truth leaves us exposed and guilty before God, who judges us in righteousness. But the truth also invites us to deliverance, to change, and to life.

In Luke 19:1-10, we have a great story of a human life transformed by divine love. The closing words of this passage (vv. 9-10) sum up the mission of Jesus Christ.

> *And Jesus said unto him, This day is salvation come to this house, forasmuch as he also is a son of Abraham. For the Son of man is come to seek and to save that which was lost.*

Zacchaeus was a short man. He is described as "little of stature." But he was short in other ways than feet and inches, ways that mattered more.

He was short of friends. Tax collectors were hated by the public, especially Jewish tax collectors who worked for the Roman government. When Zacchaeus wanted to see Jesus, the crowd refused to open a path to the roadside. They closed ranks and elbowed the hated man to the rear.

He was short of character. Like other revenue collectors of his day and place, he had enriched himself by exploiting others. The tax system allowed for extortion, and the collectors took full advantage of the system.

And he was short of opportunity. Jesus "passed through Jericho," as verse 1 says, and He never returned. Opportunity is

59

dynamic, not static. It passes, and a person has to seize it or lose it, perhaps lose it forever. This is why the gospel invitation is sounded with such urgency in the Scriptures: "Come now!"

II. **Zacchaeus was a sought man.** Not by the crowd, for they despised him. But Jesus came to seek the lost, so we read that "Jesus came to the place" where Zacchaeus was perched in a tree to get a view of the road.

Jesus braved the slander of the crowd in His quest for Zacchaeus. He invited himself home for dinner with the most hated man in town. Religious folks were shocked, saying, "He has gone to be guest with . . . a sinner." Why, He could have dined with the ministerial association! Instead, He broke bread with a crooked politician.

That is just like Jesus! As the doctor visits the sick, so the Savior calls on the lost. A man isn't known by the company he keeps—that's a lie the church keeps repeating to its own shame. A man is known for the reason he keeps company. And Jesus' reason for keeping company with Zacchaeus brings us to the happiest part of the story.

III. **Zacchaeus became a saved man.** During dinner he jumped to his feet, declared his independence from the idol of greed, and promised to make restitution for money gotten through crooked means. And Jesus said, "This day is salvation come to this house."

Zacchaeus was not saved by his works but by his faith. Helping the poor would not save him. Restoring stolen money would not save him. He became a true son of Abraham, the man who was "justified by faith," the man who "believed God, and it was counted unto him for righteousness" (Rom. 3:28; 4:3; see Gal. 3:6). Zacchaeus trusted in the God who justifies the ungodly, who graciously pardons sinners when they repent.

That is the story of Zacchaeus, summed up in three words: short, sought, saved. Your name may not be Zack, but

60

you need the Lord Jesus, too. You may be a taxpayer, not a tax collector, but unless you repent you will go to hell as surely as any corrupt politician, ancient or modern. You may not be short in stature, but a fellow tall enough to play center in pro basketball can be as deep in sin and as far from God as a wicked midget.

You don't have to be lost. Jesus seeks you out, just as He did Zacchaeus. *If you will do what Zacchaeus did, receive Jesus joyfully, He will save you from sin.* He will transform your life and repair its broken relationships. He will give you freedom and joy that money can't buy.

Listen again to our Lord's words as He declares the purpose of His life, death, and resurrection: "For the Son of man is come to seek and to save that which was lost." There is hope for the person who will respond, "That's me, O Lord, that's me!" Or if your grammar is better than your life, "That's I, O Lord, that's I."

One more thing: Zacchaeus "made haste" to receive Jesus. *You have no time to lose and a soul to save.* Act now!

O Jesus, Lord and Savior, how glad we are that You came to seek and save us. We could never find You if You didn't find us first. You alone can save us. Do it now! Amen.

Jesus, the Stone

Let's take a very serious Bible break today. I refer to Luke 20:9-19. Check these words in verses 17 and 18:

> *And he beheld them, and said, What is this then that is written, The stone which the builders rejected, the same is become the head of the corner? Whosoever shall fall upon that stone shall be broken; but on whomsoever it shall fall, it will grind him to powder.*

Jesus Christ is a stone, a cornerstone. Unless one's life is founded on Him and held together by Him, it is doomed to fail. It's just that simple. Every life not built upon Jesus will be destroyed forever. For "other foundation can no man lay," and no man laid this one—God did it!

We have two choices, friend, and that is all. We can fall on this stone and be broken, or the stone will fall on us and we will be destroyed.

Falling on Christ, the Stone, will break us to pieces.

He shatters our *pride*. In his sinful pride man likes to think he can be his own savior. He likes to think his own life is good enough for God to accept and reward. But that's sheer folly. Any man who thinks his life should be pleasing to an infinitely holy God is lying to himself or lying about himself. "All have sinned," and pride must be broken if we are to be saved from sin.

Falling on the Stone will also break our *will*. Man's first sin was the opposition of his will to the will of God. When sin is boiled down and skimmed off, its distilled essence is rebellion against God. Man wants to be god over his own life.

He comes to God like the prodigal first came to his father, saying, *"Give me."* Then he squanders the goodness of God on his own lusts. We will never find the trail back from the hogpen to home until, like the prodigal son, we come to the Father, saying, *"Make me."* Our wills must be surrendered.

Yes, falling on the Stone will break us to pieces. But listen! *Jesus picks up the pieces and makes something beautiful from them.* The devil delights in taking a whole man and breaking him to pieces, but the Lord delights in taking the pieces and making him whole again. He takes those who are in pieces and says, "Go in peace." Peace is wholeness.

But what if you don't fall on the Stone? What if you refuse to cast yourself on the mercy of Christ? Then the Stone will fall on you!

II — **Christ, the Stone, falling on us, crushes us to powder.**

Jesus will have mercy on every penitent sinner. That is the message of the gospel. But it is just as true that Jesus will bring judgment on every sinner who refuses to repent. No teaching is plainer in the Book of God than the message of judgment and wrath on the finally impenitent. Those who deny this hard truth are closing their eyes to "the whole counsel of God."

Jesus said, "Come unto me, all you that labour and are heavy laden, and I will give you rest" (Matt. 11:28). But this same Jesus represents himself as the final Judge of all men, and to some of them He will say, "Depart from me, you cursed, into everlasting fire." *To affirm the Christ of mercy but deny the Christ of judgment is another expression of man's rebellion against God.*

We fall on the Stone and are broken in pieces, but Christ makes something valuable of the pieces. But if the Stone falls on us, it grinds us to powder, and He makes nothing from that powder!

There is a clear and terrible alternative before us in the

Bible. It is life or death, heaven or hell. It is being broken by repentance or being crushed by judgment. What is your choice today?

In many churches there can be found a very special item of furniture. It is called by some "the mourner's bench," by others "the penitent form," by others "the altar of prayer." Some ecclesiastical snobs have ridiculed it, but it symbolizes the truth that God saves the contrite, those who mourn over their sins and pray to be forgiven. At such altars thousands of broken people have found the healing pardon of Jesus Christ. But other thousands have made their altars at home, or even in their automobiles. Wherever you are right now, as you read this, you can fall upon Christ, be broken and mended, and discover new life!

O God, You have set a Stone in our world on which life will be builded or by which life will be destroyed. Let us fall upon the Stone, be broken and healed and saved. In Jesus' name. Amen.

Beyond the Empty Tomb—Forgiveness

Easter is the most exciting day of the year for those who follow Jesus Christ. The heart of the gospel message is the resurrection of Jesus. The foundation of Christian experience is the resurrection of Jesus.

These facts are given emphasis in Luke 24:37-53. Give attention to this record of a meeting between the risen Jesus and His disciples, especially to verses 45-48.

> *Then opened he their understanding, that they might understand the scriptures, and said unto them, Thus it is written, and thus it behoved Christ to suffer, and to rise from the dead the third day: and that repentance and remission of sins should be preached in his name among all nations, beginning at Jerusalem. And you are witnesses of these things.*

Repentance is a human act, a turning from sin to God. Forgiveness is a divine act, the free pardon of all our sins. One waits upon the other, but both depend upon the saving action of God in the death and resurrection of Jesus Christ.

From this passage in Luke three truths emerge which have abiding validity.

The first is this: **The resurrection of Christ assures the possibility of repentance and forgiveness.**

Repentance and forgiveness can be proclaimed because, and only because, "it behoved Christ to suffer, and to rise from the dead." Christ suffered to atone for our sins. According to Paul, in a great passage on resurrection, the first element of the gospel is, "Christ died for our sins" (1 Cor. 15:3). Jesus said, "Thus it is written." One place where it is written is Isaiah 53. There we read, "The Lord has laid on him the iniquity of us all," and again, "You shall make his soul an offering for sin" (vv. 6, 10). The death of Jesus was an atonement for sin. To read another meaning into the Cross is to misread it.

Yes, Jesus died to atone for our sins, and He was raised in demonstration of the validity and power of that sacrifice. By the resurrection God declares that the sacrifice is accepted, and a power to produce repentance and assure forgiveness has been set loose in the world. We who were driving toward hell can make U-turns! God will forgive us for Jesus' sake. That is the glorious possibility opened to us through the resurrection of Jesus Christ.

II - A second truth is vitally connected to the first one: **The possibility of repentance and forgiveness is the authorized message of the Church.**

According to the Lord of the Church, "Repentance and remission of sins should be preached in his name." To these great saving truths the Church is to function as "witnesses" —proclaiming them after experiencing them. The message of the Church is a "given," and it must not be altered or exchanged. To do so is to profane the gospel and to repudiate the Lordship of Jesus Christ.

On the very day I prepared this Bible break, the local paper carried the story of a "church" that in its Sunday service had celebrated certain well-known people who died in 1980. The music of the Beatles filled the sanctuary, and a woman mimicked Mae West. To call that worship is an insult to Christ. Christian worship celebrates the one death and resurrection that makes possible our deliverance from sin. Any other message is a false gospel, a blasphemy of Christ, and a mockery of human need.

66

III — A third truth emerging from this account in Luke is this: **Repentance and forgiveness may be the experience of all to whom the message of the church comes.**

Read again these heartening words: "Repentance and remission of sins should be preached in his name among all nations." Jesus was born a Jew, but He died for all mankind. His resurrection opens the door of new life for people everywhere. The whole world has been made the beneficiary of His death on the Cross. Salvation is a global possibility.

Let's bring the Good News closer to home. As you encounter the gospel now, *you* can repent, *you* can be forgiven, *you* can be reconciled to God. For you Jesus died. For you Jesus rose again. To you He now offers His blood-bought and power-packed remission of sins. He calls you to repent. He invites you to come. The next move is yours!

A great Christian was found upon his knees before a crucifix, exclaiming in awe, "For me, for me." Paul felt that same kind of wonder, calling himself the "chief" of sinners (1 Tim. 1:15) and "less than the least of all saints" (Eph. 3:8). That we can be saved is overwhelming good news.

O risen Lord, we praise You for the love that took You to the Cross, and for the power that brought You from the grave. Let that love and power inspire our repentance and channel Your forgiveness. Amen!

The Ladder

Is your Bible covered with dust? I hope not, but it is the "best sold and worst read" book in the world. Let me ask a pointed question. Is your Sears catalogue dog-eared and worn, while your Bible still looks new after 10 years? Read John 1:43-51. We find these words spoken by Jesus:

> *Verily, verily, I say unto you, Hereafter you shall see heaven open, and the angels of God ascending and descending upon the Son of man* (v. 51).

That "verily, verily" has tremendous significance as a witness to Jesus. There are 25 places in John's Gospel where a saying of Jesus begins with "Verily, verily, I say unto you." This is the first such occurrence. This way of introducing His words marks Jesus off from all other men who ever taught in Israel. The rabbis never began, "Verily, verily"—or as the Greek text reads, "Amen, amen." The rabbis quoted the Word of God, some Old Testament saying, and then added an Amen. That added Amen was their way of saying, "God's Word is true, and let it be so for us." Even the prophets could only begin their messages with, "Thus says the Lord." Prophets did not say, "I say to you." But Jesus did! *Unlike all the rabbis and prophets, He spoke with direct personal authority:* "Amen, amen, I say unto you."

This fact gives the lie to all the polite blasphemy that reduces Jesus to a mere rabbi or prophet. He was a rabbi, He was a prophet, but infinitely more. That "more" is given right here in Nathanael's words in verse 49: "Rabbi, you are the Son of God." *Jesus was more than a man speaking for God. He was God speaking to men.* A fellow who says Jesus was only a man, a rabbi, a prophet—well, verily, verily, he doesn't know what verily, verily means!

Look at the saying of Jesus which is prefaced by this solemn and authoritative formula: "You shall see heaven open, and the angels of God ascending and descending upon the Son of man." These words of Jesus recall the dream of Jacob, recorded in Gen. 28:12. Jacob was camping out on his first night away from home. He laid his head on a rock and had a strange dream. He saw a ladder reaching from earth to heaven, and angels were going up and down the ladder. The Lord stood above it and made some great covenant promises to sinful, undeserving Jacob.

Jesus is saying, "I am Jacob's Ladder. I am the Connection between heaven and earth, between God and people. Through me, the blessings of God are mediated to you." This is the truth that stirred Paul to write, "There is one God, and one mediator between God and men, the man Christ Jesus; who gave himself a ransom for all" (1 Tim. 2:5-6).

Friend, *that ladder is the gospel—it is the Good News!* Sin put a chasm between God and men. Heaven and earth were disconnected. But in Jesus Christ, who died for our sins, reconciliation has been effected. The gulf has been bridged. Heaven and earth are joined again. God's blessings can reach us now.

And that ladder is grace—it has been set up by God, not by man. We cannot reach God by our own efforts. We cannot find God by our groping and searching. All our philosophies and religions are short ladders, reaching only to failure and frustration. But God's ladder is long enough. His ladder was set up by the incarnation, crucifixion, and resurrection of Jesus: "The Father sent the Son to be the Saviour of the world" (1 John 4:14).

The angels of God use that ladder, but they are not the ladder. Angels can no more save us than we can save ourselves. Angels are messengers. That is the meaning of the word "angels" in the mother tongue of the New Testament. They run a delivery service for God. But only Jesus, the Rabbi who is more than a rabbi, who is the Son of God and the Son of Man, can save us from sin.

The first and foremost gift that reaches us across God's ladder is salvation. His ladder is a ladder of life, a ladder of hope. It is God's way to us for salvation, and it is our way to God for communion.

You can make a ladder of your own, but it won't work. You can borrow a ladder from some guru, or spiritualist, or astrologer, or religious leader, but it won't work. All you will get for your climbing is a broken neck. God's ladder is Jesus. He is the "verily, verily" of God and the one hope of mankind. You don't have to climb up to Him, He has come down to you. He offers you the gifts of an open heaven, gracious pardon, and eternal life. Receive Him in faith and obedience today!

We thank You, O God, for Your ladder, Jesus Christ. Send Your blessings down in the measure of our needs and for the glory of His name. And we will send our praises up from grateful, redeemed hearts. Amen.

Wealth and Power

Slide your coffee cup over and make room for your Bible. Open it to the Book of Acts. Read chapters 2 and 3, and underscore verse 6 in chapter 3.

Then Peter said, Silver and gold have I none; but such as I have I give you: In the name of Jesus Christ of Nazareth rise up and walk.

Here we have a combination of the usual and the unusual.

I — *It is usual for preachers to be broke.* Many of them get salaries that rabbits couldn't live on if carrots were a dime a bunch. By the time they feed the youngsters, dress the wife, support the church, put gas in the car, and pay traffic tickets, there is nothing left. If a few dollars should remain, Internal Revenue Service sucks them up like a sponge drinking soup. There is nothing more ordinary than a preacher saying, "Silver and gold have I none."

II — *But it is unusual to hear one say, "In the name of Jesus, rise up and walk."* Peter was broke, but he tapped a gold mine—all the resources of love and power that are represented by "the name of Jesus." When he put those resources to work in the situation, the beggar was soon "walking, and leaping, and praising God." That, my friend, is the description of a holy jig!

Too many preachers have lost confidence in the name of Jesus Christ. They can't seem to take the Lord at His word and trust Him to do what the Bible claims He can do. And you just watch it—*when a preacher shrinks his Christ he enlarges other people.* My, the name-dropping that goes on in many

71

sermons! The name of this bigwig theologian and that hot-shot psychiatrist has the preacher's trust instead of Jesus Christ. But nothing is happening. The beggar is still sitting there with a hand out and a dazed look in his eyes. I tell you, Geritol can do more to help people than some preachers think Jesus can do for them!

What is wrong? Well, rest your eyes for a moment on verse 1. It looks like a clue: "Peter and John went up together into the temple at the hour of prayer." Prayer! Here is the problem. *There is little faith because there is little prayer.* Prayer and faith are like Siamese twins joined at the heart—separate them and both die. When we don't pray we can't say, "Rise up and walk." We can only say, "Sit there and die." Or, "Move over, I'll flop down and die with you."

Perhaps the lack of prayer is not the whole problem. Maybe it's just a symptom, and the sickness has a deeper cause. Look back into chapter 2. There at verse 4 we read something very important about these apostles: "And they were all filled with the Holy Spirit." *Spirit-filled men are praying men, and praying men are believing men.* That is the whole chain from which this miracle hangs.

And look at these words in verse 14 of chapter 2: "But Peter, standing up with the eleven . . ." When the Holy Spirit got Peter on his feet, he could say to the beggar, "Rise up and walk." Now come back to Acts 3. Verse 7 says, "He took him by the right hand, and lifted him up." Peter could pull the beggar up because Peter was already standing up. *A church on its back cannot lift the world to its feet.* A sick church cannot rescue a dying world. Only Spirit-filled, praying, trusting Christians can utilize the vast resources of Jesus' name.

What tremendous resources are there! I could sign my name to a check for a million dollars, but it would bounce higher than the church steeple. I could even sign it "Rockefeller," and I would not get anything for it, unless it was 20 years in the penitentiary for forgery. But you and I have been given access to the wealth of Christ's love and power. His name is the difference between defeat and victory, between bondage and freedom, between death and life. Think of it!

Christian friend, are you filled with the Spirit? Are you a man or woman given to prayer? Do you believe in the power of Jesus Christ to transform human situations? Are you ready to take lost and broken people by the hand and give them a lift into new life? The promise of the Spirit's infilling and enablement is for you today!

Unsaved friend, are you just sitting there, unable to cope with your sin and guilt and condemnation? Are you trying everyone and everything but Jesus, leaving yourself still beggared and lost? Our Lord loves you as much as He has ever loved anyone, and He is just as willing and able to save you as He has ever been to save anyone. He can free you from sin and give you new life if you will trust Him.

O Christ, help us to depend upon Your name, not upon our brains or bank accounts. Don't let our churches and preachers become materially rich but spiritually bankrupt. Let us be Spirit-filled people who can pray and act in faith. Amen.

Faith

The 16th chapter of Acts tells an exciting story. Missionaries Paul and Silas had been arrested, beaten, and flung into a dungeon. At midnight the intrepid pair "prayed and sang praises unto God." An earthquake shook the prison; doors flew open and chains fell off. The jailer, awakened from sleep and thinking the prisoners had escaped, started to kill himself. Paul stopped him, shouting, "We are all here." Then the jailer, trembling in fear of God, asked,

What must I do to be saved?

Paul answered,

Believe on the Lord Jesus Christ, and you will be saved, and your house (vv. 30-31).

A happy scene follows as the jailer tenderly washes the wounds of Paul and Silas, feeds them a hearty meal, and listens to "the word of the Lord" which they eagerly proclaim.

Spend a few minutes now, thinking about this old story and its message for us.

I— *Consider, first, the question:* "What must I do to be saved?" That's the most important question the jailer—or anyone else—ever asked.

Lesser questions are more frequently asked. Multitudes are asking, "What must I do to make money?" "What must I do to lose weight?" "What must I do to be successful in my career?" "What must I do to be popular with my peers?" "What must I do to have fun?" In their time and place these questions are legitimate, but they are not most important!

74

Their concern is with the transient, not the eternal, issues of life.

More than anything else man needs to be right with God, to be saved from sin, to have hope of eternal life. And that makes the jailer's question one that everybody needs to raise, and to raise seriously and urgently.

II — Listen again to the *answer:* "Believe on the Lord Jesus Christ, and you will be saved." We are saved by faith in Jesus Christ, or we are not saved at all. God has one plan only for rescuing us from sin, death, and hell. That one way of salvation is by faith in Jesus Christ.

We are to believe *in* Him, not simply believe something *about* Him. We are not saved by reciting creeds, however orthodox, but by trusting in Jesus Christ. *Right opinions have no more power to save than empty rituals.* "The devils believe," in the sense of mental assent to truth, but they are not saved (James 2:19).

We are to believe on Jesus Christ, and not another. There is but one way to God, the Christ who said, "I am the way, the truth, and the life: no man comes unto the Father but by me" (John 14:6). We may respect other men for the depth of their thought or the heroism of their deeds, but no one can save us from sin and reconcile us to God but Jesus Christ.

Believe in Him and you will be saved! Believe in someone else, and you may be reformed, or educated, or civilized, or stimulated to great actions and noble sacrifices, but you will not be saved from sin.

Believe in Jesus Christ and you will be saved from the *guilt* of sin. All your sins will be freely forgiven, for His sake.

Believe in Jesus Christ and you will be saved from the *grip* of sin. He will free you from its power and dominion. He will free you to be a different person and to live a different life, no longer paralyzed by guilt and enslaved by habit, but walking in joy as the child of God.

III — And that brings us to another thought: *The question, the answer, and then the **result**.* The jailer was baptized "and rejoiced, believing in God with all his house."

Jesus brings joy! "There is joy in the presence of the angels of God over one sinner who repents" (Luke 15:10). And there is joy in the heart of that sinner who repents and believes in the Lord Jesus Christ! The happiest people on the face of our sorrow-saturated earth are the people who have trusted in Jesus for their salvation.

I have preached for many years in many places, and I have talked with lots of people who are sad because they refused to come to Jesus and be saved. But I have yet to find anyone, anywhere, who regretted giving his life to the Lord. Jesus saves, and when He saves He creates joy!

Lord Jesus Christ, You alone can save. From futile trust in ourselves or others, deliver us, we pray. May the jailer's question and the apostle's answer be personal experience for us all. Amen!

Your Response to God

Let me ask you a very direct question. Are you right with God? Have you been saved from sin? Do you know Jesus as your personal Savior?

Do yourself a favor. Get your Bible and read Acts 17:22-34. Here is the record of a sermon preached by Paul in Athens—not the whole sermon, likely, but a careful synopsis. What a message it was! *He stormed the citadel of idolatry:* "We ought not to think that the Godhead is like unto gold, or silver, or stone, graven by art and man's device." *He thundered a call to repentance:* "God . . . now commands all men every where to repent." *He warned of future judgment:* "He has appointed a day, in the which He will judge the world in righteousness . . ." It was tender, rugged preaching.

The response of his listeners is recorded in verses 32-34:

> *And when they heard of the resurrection of the dead, some mocked: and others said, We will hear you again of this matter. So Paul departed from among them. Howbeit certain men clave unto him, and believed.*

Here are three responses to the gospel, the only three that can be made. You will make one of them! And eternal destiny depends upon your personal response to the Word of God.

1. "Some mocked." *This was the response of the **hard-hearted.*** In their pride of intellect, in their love for sin, they treated the Word of God as a joke. They had no more respect for the gospel than a modern has for a comic strip. Sin, repentance, judgment—to them it was nonsense! They had created a god

77

in their own image, and their god was unconcerned about sin, demanded no repentance, and scheduled no judgment.

Well, many a fool has mocked his way to hell, but no one ever scoffed his way back from hell. "God is not mocked," not ultimately, for a man reaps what he sows (Gal. 6:7). Sow mockery and you will reap damnation. "The wages of sin is death" (Rom. 6:23). Mocking the gospel is like tearing up the only prescription that can save you from a fatal illness.

II — "Others said, we will hear you again." *This was the response of the halfhearted.* Mockers said, "No." These people said, "Later." They took the attitude that it may be true but it is not urgent. Other matters concern us more. We have other fish to fry. When it's convenient we will hear you again.

And the next thing we read is, "So Paul departed." He packed his bags and headed out. The meeting was over. Paul knew that "later" was rebellion against God as surely as "no." Nothing is more important than a man's relationship to God. To brush aside the gospel and go home to read the sports page is moral idiocy.

God never says "later," never says "tomorrow." Read the Bible and see. Every command to repent, every invitation to faith, is expressed in the languge of immediacy and urgency. "Come now . . ." "The Holy Spirit says, Today . . ." No one can quit sin too soon or find God too early. If we were as smart in the spiritual realm as we are in the material realm we would flee from sin and come to Christ quicker than we would clear a burning barn.

III — Some mocked, some delayed. "Howbeit certain men . . . believed." *This is the response of the hungry-hearted.* Then and there they turned from sin and trusted in Jesus Christ.

You can turn back one chapter and find out what happens when a person believes. The Philippian jailer, smitten with conviction, fell before Paul and Silas exclaiming, "What must I do to be saved?" The answer came as quick and clear as light: "Believe on the Lord Jesus Christ, and you will be saved." Jesus died and rose again to save us from sin. When we trust in Him we are forgiven and life blossoms anew.

A woman, weary of life and thinking of suicide, stood on a street corner awaiting a bus. From a nearby church she heard joyful singing. Drawn by curiosity and hunger she entered the church and heard the gospel. She said yes to its invitation and promise, and became a radiant Christian. She served in faith and died in hope. Not even cancer could quench the joy she had in Christ. What He did for her He will do for you.

There are three things you can say to God when He calls you through the gospel: "no," "later," and "yes." Saying "no" is *mad,* for God is not mocked. Saying "later" is *sad,* for you can wait too long and lose your opportunity forever. Saying "yes" is *glad,* for it brings pardon and peace from God. What is your answer? Your destiny hinges upon it! Say yes to life today!

O God, be no longer an "unknown God." Reveal yourself in Jesus, who died and rose again. Forgive our sins, smash our idols, and make us Yours. And do it now, Lord, as we say yes to Your offer of eternal life in Jesus' name. Amen.

The Whole Truth

Good-byes can be very sad. I see lots of good-byes taking place in airports as I travel to and from my preaching missions. Sometimes those who are saying farewell speak truths that will be cherished forever. In the Book of Acts, 20:17-38, we have such a farewell recorded. Paul was making his last visit to the elders of the church at Ephesus. It is a passage full of pathos, for Paul knew that he would likely never see them again, and they were dear to his heart as he was to theirs. In verses 26-28 we find a truth that endured the grief and speaks to our hearts today:

> Wherefore I take you to record this day, that I am pure from the blood of all men. For I have not shunned to declare unto you all the counsel of God. Take heed therefore unto yourselves.

I— **We need "all the counsel of God."**

We need the whole range of divine truth by which men are saved and by which they must live. As Jesus put it, "Man shall not live by bread alone, but by every word that proceeds out of the mouth of God" (Matt. 4:4). In this way alone can we be sure to avoid every evil and practice every good.

Now, we may not *want* the whole counsel of God. We may prefer to shield our consciences from some of its blows. The Bible packs a mightier wallop than a steam hammer. We would like to ignore those teachings of the Word that expose our sins, challenge our prejudices, and shame our compromises. It is an uncomfortable experience to sit under the full glare of the Bible's light. Like a guilty prisoner with a light in his face we can only confess or cover up.

II — Whether we want "all the counsel of God" or not, someone will declare it to us.

Some won't, of course. Some preachers work on this principle: Find out what people want to hear and tell them that. But about the time these prophets of the status quo make us comfortable, along comes an Elijah to trouble Israel, or a Nathan to say, "You are the man" (2 Sam. 12:7), or a Paul determined to keep his hands "pure from the blood" of lost people. Then the truth will come out, and the light will shine, and our hiding places will be uncovered.

But that is only because God loves us too much to let us be deceived, even self-deceived. Like a faithful doctor, He probes and cuts, not because He takes pleasure in our pain, but because He wants us to be healed. *He makes us whole persons by His whole counsel.* So He sends along faithful witnesses who will not lie, and they preach both love and wrath, both mercy and judgment, both promise and demand, both heaven and hell. They forbid us to pick and choose among the truths of Scripture. They apply its full range of teaching to our full range of needs.

Paul knew that he would take the record of his ministry to the Judgment. He did not want blood on his hands because he had been silent on unpopular subjects. That leads us to another fact implied in this passage:

III — When we hear "all the counsel of God" we become accountable for living in its light.

"Take heed therefore unto yourselves!" We take heed by resolute obedience to the truth. John puts it like this: "If we walk in the light, as he is in the light, we have fellowship one with another, and the blood of Jesus Christ his Son cleanses us from all sin" (1 John 1:7). *Light isn't to stare at, it's to walk in.*

81

Paul's warning was not wasted breath. He knew that where the light had shined the devil would be busy trying to put it out. He warns that "wolves" will enter the flock—wolves clothed as sheep; and even some church leaders would end up "speaking perverse things, to draw away disciples after them." The security of the flock lies in "the word of his grace" which edifies and sanctifies.

We will be held responsible for the truth we have received. The gospel that we hear now will confront us again—at the Judgment. *We will account for the light of the Word in the light of the Judgment.* This doesn't mean that ignorance of the Word will excuse our sins. God holds us accountable for seeking opportunities to hear His truth. We will answer, not only for the light we had, but for the light we could have had. Dodging the Word of God is wicked, just as hearing but disobeying it is evil. Let us "buy the truth, and sell it not" (Prov. 23:23)!

Are you walking in the light? Have you obeyed all the truth that God has brought to you from the Bible? Are you living by every word that proceeds from the mouth of God? Are you translating into practice "all the counsel of God"?

God of truth and light and grace, we thank You for Your Word. It lays bare our sin and guilt, but it points us to the cleansing in Christ's blood. It shines on our pathway to light our feet to heaven. Help us to cherish the truth, to walk in the light, to live by Your words! In Jesus' name. Amen.

82

An Imprisoned Judge

Have you thought about God today? Have you talked to God today? Have you heard from God today? Nothing is more important, because "in him we live, and move, and have our being" (Acts 17:28). Life comes from Him and goes to Him. Money, property, family—we will leave them all sooner or later, but we will never get away from God.

This being true, how vital it is to consult God's Word! There is a passage in the Book of Acts that I want to share with you: 24:24-27. The 25th verse is probably quite familiar:

> And as he reasoned of righteousness, temperance, and judgment to come, Felix trembled, and answered, Go your way for this time; when I have a convenient season, I will call for you.

Paul knew the inside of more jails than a maladroit bank robber. His only crime was loving people and preaching Christ, but he was often put on trial for that. This time his judge was a Roman official named Felix.

At the hearing Paul spoke of "the faith in Christ." Warming to his subject, Paul "reasoned" about justice, self-control, and future judgment. Think of it! He preached about judgment to the judge! Paul had a ton of courage.

Felix was corrupt, as many ancient and modern politicians have been, and the preaching poleaxed his conscience. He "trembled." But a man is not saved by shaking. James tells us that demons believe and tremble, but they go right on being demons. And Felix went right on being a sinner for all his trembling. He got Paul off his back by sending

83

him back to jail with the promise, "When I have a convenient season, I will call for you." Convenient season—that was malarkey! He had time then and there to quit his meanness and come to Christ, but he was unwilling to break with sin. *Felix, the judge, was bound tighter than Paul, the prisoner.*

I — **Felix was bound by fear of men.** Look at verse 27: "Desiring to do the Jews a favor, Felix left Paul in prison" (paraphrase). It's an old and sad story—give the people what they want. Never mind what is just and true, do what is expedient. Don't make enemies. Curry the favor of those who can set you up or knock you down.

Fear of men has caused moral havoc in the world and church. It spawns compromise of conscience and rejection of Christ. Only God knows how many have trembled under conviction but remained in their sins, chained by their fear of what others might think, say, or do if they became Christians.

II — **Felix was bound, too, by love for money.** Look at verse 26: "He hoped also that money would be given him by Paul." Felix was a money-grubbing governor. He knew Paul was innocent, but he kept him in jail. He thought, If I let him cool his heels in a cell long enough, surely he will try to bribe his way out. Felix was dead wrong. Paul would not play that game.

Money, money, money—how many has it damned? Some folks want money so badly they will do anything to get their greedy paws on it. They will pervert justice, pull crooked business deals, falsify tax reports—anything. Worst of all, they will reject "the faith in Christ" if it threatens their money supply.

III — **Felix was bound, also, by lust for evil.** Paul's preaching was on target. He "reasoned of righteousness, temperance, and judgment to come," and Felix was unrighteous, undisciplined, and unprepared for judgment. God doesn't shoot blanks.

But Felix enjoyed his wickedness. He wanted more of it. The thought of judgment spoiled the pleasures of sin, so he silenced the preacher. He wanted to stop shaking and get back to sinning. Felix was not unusual. Thousands who hear the gospel are sinning it away. They are drowning the voice of conscience in their cocktails. They are silencing the voice of the gospel with their rock and roll music.

"A convenient season"? Neighbor, we cannot dictate to a sovereign God. We will be saved on His terms and at His time, or we will surely miss heaven. "Behold, now is the accepted time; behold, now is the day of salvation" (2 Cor. 6:2). If you are not ready for judgment, I urge you to get on your prayer bones and ask God to save you. *You cannot afford to let people, money, or sin become the price tag on a damned soul.*

Lord, the only convenient season we have is now. The only breath we are sure of is what fills our lungs now. We must not postpone this most important of all matters. Save us now. Forgive us, cleanse us, renew us, so that we can live righteously and temperately and in readiness for judgment. In Jesus' name. Amen.

Remember the Poor

Scratch around in that pile of magazines yonder and find your Bible. Open it to Paul's letter to the Galatians, and read chapter 2. Notice as you read that Paul had some problems and quarrels in the church to resolve. So what's new? Now concentrate your attention on verse 10:

Only they would that we should remember the poor: the same which I also was forward to do.

The Church has never been perfect. Early Christians had their differences, just as today's Christians do. Racial tensions and religious arguments marred the Church's life then just as they do now. But on one thing the Church was agreed. They agreed that being a vital Christian means caring for the poor.

I — **Jesus Christ remembered the poor.** When He preached in His hometown synagogue He said, "The Spirit of the Lord is upon me, because he has anointed me to preach the gospel to the poor" (Luke 4:18). And in His ministry Jesus brought healing and bread, along with the gospel message, to the poor.

II — **His first followers remembered the poor.** Paul tells us that the "pillars" of the church did this, and they urged him to do it. He asserts, "I was *forward* to do" it.

If we are going to be Christians today, we cannot be backward where the Early Church was forward. This is no time to put Christianity into reverse gear. You and I are responsible to our Lord for the care of the poor.

"Remember the poor" in your prayers. Well-fixed and well-known people never lack for someone to pray for them.

86

But who bears to God in prayer the names and needs of the poor of earth? Blessed are you, friend, if you can say, "I do."

God is interested in the poor. The Bible, from cover to cover, represents Him as the Champion of the needy. The harshest words in the Bible are God's condemnation of the rich who exploit and oppress the poor. And to the poor who will turn to Him, God gives gracious promises and privileges. As James wrote, "Has not God chosen the poor of this world rich in faith, and heirs of the kingdom which he has promised to them that love him?" (James 2:5).

You may be sure that when you pray for the poor you get the ear of God, for He cares deeply about them.

"Remember the poor" with your money. Praying is not enough. I mentioned it first for good reason, though. If you will pray for the poor, God will impress you to answer some of your own prayers. When you care enough to pray you will care enough to give. That's how it works.

I am not suggesting that it works automatically. Some pray for the lost who never tell anyone about the Savior. And some pray for the poor who never spend a dollar to help relieve their misery. Prayer can be a substitute for doing and giving, but that's only when people and prayer are insincere. Honest prayers become generous givers.

Being a Christian means vastly more than passing out religious tracts and preaching to folks. It has to do with more than "spiritual" work. Being a Christian means things like buying food for hungry people. And paying rent to keep a widow from being evicted from her house. And footing the bill for medicine so a sick man can get back on his feet and go back to his job. In God's sight, this kind of compassion is worth more than all the stained-glass windows and frescoed walls and plaster saints in the world. "Pure religion and undefiled before God and the Father is this, To visit the fatherless and widows in their affliction, and to keep himself unspotted from the world" (James 1:27).

"Remember the poor," too, by your influence. We need Christians who will pressure lawmakers to enact and enforce legislation that relieves the burdens of the poor. We need Christians who will pressure business leaders to create jobs, and better-paying jobs, to help the poor. We need Christians who will speak out against the heartless crooks in government, business, and religion who exploit the poor for their own advantage. The poor are well nigh helpless to defend themselves or to improve their lot. They need friends at court and friends in Congress and friends in the Church.

The heart of Jesus Christ was burdened for the poor. Unless it is plain to the world that the Church cares for the poor, the Church is betraying its Lord.

When we talk about the Church, we are really talking about you and me! What are we doing for the poor?

O Lord, help us to remember the poor. Help our hearts to be burdened with those who burden Your heart. In our prayers, with our money, and by our influence, help us to be the champions of the helpless. In the name of Him who became poor for our sakes. Amen.

Forgiveness

Our Bible break today will be taken in Ephesians. In the opening chapter of this letter the apostle Paul sets forth the riches of our "spiritual blessings . . . in Christ." Over and over rings the phrase "in him." In Him we have been chosen, accepted, adopted, and gathered together. In Him we have obtained an inheritance, which is heaven.

Of all the blessings we have in Christ, this is the very greatest:

> In [him] we have redemption through his blood, the forgiveness of sins, according to the riches of his grace (v. 7).

The forgiveness of sins! To those who have felt the burden of guilt, to those who have stood self-accused and self-condemned, filled with bitter memories and vast regrets, the forgiveness of sins is the most liberating, joyful experience possible.

If you have been forgiven, let this passage rekindle the flames of joy and praise in your heart. If you have not been forgiven, let God assure you of His pardoning love today.

I.— **The ground of forgiveness is set forth here:** "In [him] . . . through his blood . . . according to the riches of his grace."

The ground of our forgiveness is "in him," never in us. We can be forgiven because of what He has done for us, not because of what we have done for Him.

What has He done? "Christ died for our sins" (1 Cor. 15:3). God has decreed that "without shedding of blood is no remission" (Heb. 9:22), and the blood of Jesus became our offering for sin, our sacrifice of atonement. God accepted that offering and demonstrated His acceptance by raising Jesus from the dead. God will forgive all who come to Him claiming forgiveness on no other basis but the blood of Jesus. Forgiveness cannot be earned; it can only be received as the gift of God. The whole ground of our forgiveness is the Cross!

II — **The effect of forgiveness is also set forth in Paul's words.** "In him we have redemption through his blood." Redemption! In all the vocabulary of religion there is not a sweeter word. Redemption is liberation, the rescue of the captive, the release of the slave.

Sin enslaves. Guilt forges chains for the human spirit, binding man in a hell of fear and self-contempt. Habits of sin fasten upon him, forcing him to repeat his sins when they no longer produce even transient pleasure. And all the efforts of a sinner to free himself are unavailing, the mere rattling of his chains and bars.

But Jesus Christ is a mighty Redeemer. "He breaks the pow'r of canceled sin; / He sets the pris'ner free." When Jesus says, "Your sins are forgiven," the paralyzing grip of our accusing past, with its repeated moral failures, is broken. We walk in newness of life. Inwardly and outwardly we are freed to be what God created us to be, men and women in happy communion with Him and at peace with one another. Forgiveness is liberating; it is redeeming.

To the woman taken in adultery, flung before Jesus by angry and heartless accusers, He said, "I do not condemn you; go, and sin no more" (see John 8:11). That is what His forgiveness means—that we can go in moral triumph and live by the truest, highest aspirations of our hearts. We no longer grovel in old, enslaving, destructive ways. Life becomes new.

Are you tired of sin, with its guilt and misery? Would you like to experience this free and freeing forgiveness? You can, and you need not wait a moment longer. Right now, if you will turn from your sins and trust in Jesus Christ, you will be forgiven and unshackled. In the words of an old hymn,

> *We who in Christ believe*
> *That He for us hath died,*
> *We all His unknown peace receive*
> *And feel His blood applied.*
> *Exults our rising soul,*
> *Disburdened of her load,*
> *And swells, unutterably full,*
> *Of glory and of God.*

"In [him] we have redemption through his blood, the forgiveness of sins, according to the riches of his grace"!

God of all grace, how can we praise You enough for Your gifts of pardon and liberation? In Jesus Christ, at awesome cost, You have provided our deliverance from sin and death. We claim that everlasting prize in His name! Amen.

The Gift of Power

The Christian life is a wonderful adventure, but it isn't an easy way. The work of the church is a thrilling achievement, but it isn't easily done. The life and work of those who follow Jesus demands a power that is more than human, a power that can only come from God. Paul writes of this power in his second letter to Timothy. Read chapter 1, and tarry over verse 7:

> God has not given us the spirit of fear; but of power, and of love, and of a sound mind.

God's gift of power can enable the weakest of us to live effective and fruitful Christian lives.

The gift of God is power to work when we are tempted to quit. Timothy's work had been difficult under the best of circumstances. He was responsible for preaching the gospel and supervising the church in a vast Asian field. Now the task was even harder, for at the time Paul wrote this letter persecution had broken out against the Church. Paul himself would soon be martyred, and men like Timothy had to keep the work going. With Christianity officially outlawed, with persecution spreading, the obstacles seemed almost insurmountable.

But God supplies a gift of power that enables the believer to work on and fight on, regardless of disheartening situations. Paul exhorts Timothy to fan into flames that gift: "Stir up the gift of God, which is in you" (v. 6). So far from giving up, he is expected to triumph in the midst of adversity and suffering: "Be [a] partaker of the affliction of the gospel

92

according to the power of God" (v. 8). *Victorious suffering has always been one of the most convincing strategies of the Christian mission.*

Are you called upon to serve the Lord in a hard place? Must you live your life and bear your witness under severe trials? There is a gift of power to appropriate which will keep you working when tempted to quit!

II — **The gift of God is power to love when we are confronted by hatred.** In Paul's day hatred for Christians had swelled into a wave of persecution. Facing this hatred, Timothy was not to retaliate, but to steadfastly love and patiently endure. To make this possible, God gives "the spirit . . . of love."

The Christian life was made possible because God loved us when we were hateful and hating, loved us enough to give His Son as a sacrifice for our sins. The Christ who said, "Love your enemies" (Matt. 5:44), was himself the demonstration of God's love for His enemies. As Paul expressed it in his letter to the Romans, "When we were enemies, we were reconciled to God by the death of his Son" (5:10). When Jesus was hanging on the Cross, mercilessly executed by His enemies, He prayed, "Father, forgive them; for they know not what they do" (Luke 23:34).

The God who loved us when we hated can enable us to love when we are hated. This love, which refuses to return evil for evil, which blesses those who revile and persecute, will be our strongest weapon for overcoming hatred and converting the haters.

III — **The gift of God is power to be calm when we are surrounded by uproar.** "God has given us the spirit . . . of a sound mind." The words suggest a sane, balanced mind, a poise and self-control in the midst of turmoil.

With persecution breaking out, Timothy could have seriously harmed his own cause by rash, panicky actions. Paul is

93

confident, however, that Timothy will keep alive the gift of balanced thinking and restrained action, leading the church wisely through perilous ways. God can make the Christian a center of calmness when everything about him is in uproar, and when men are losing their heads and acting in reckless, impulsive, damaging ways.

How vital is this gift today! Violence and hysteria are seen on every hand. The political and social and religious realms are filled with tension. Our world threatens to come apart at the seams. War talk abounds, and actual war erupts almost daily. People are cracking up, and hospitals, asylums, and jails overflow with those who could not cope. But God can fill His people with peace and power to think clearly and act calmly in the midst of these storms.

These gifts do not come to us apart from the Spirit of God. Do you need these gifts? Then God's word to you today is, "Be filled with the Spirit" (Eph. 5:18).

Our Father, we want to be at our best when the world is at its worst. We want to live wisely, lovingly, and persistently as Your representatives. For this we need Your Gift. Fill us with Your Spirit, in Christ's name! Amen.

Irreducible Christianity

Was there anything good in your mail this week? Besides junk mail and bills, there wasn't much in my box. What we all really hope for are letters. Letters are a vital part of the Bible, you know. And the letters in the New Testament are not just for those who first got them. They are for you and me.

Spend a few minutes reading Paul's letter to Titus. Chapter 1, verse 4 concludes the "hello" part of the letter. Underline it in your mind, if not in your Bible.

> To Titus, my own son after the common faith: Grace, mercy, and peace, from God the Father and the Lord Jesus Christ our Saviour.

There was a "common faith" in the early days of the Church, and there still is today. Anyone who reads the New Testament even casually knows there were differences of opinion among the first Christians. And every New Testament writer has his own slant on the faith. There is a difference of perspective and emphasis, and of language and imagery, to be found in each writer when compared to the others. But there was, at the same time, a common faith which identified and distinguished Christianity. The New Testament writers were standing in different places, overlooking different terrain, but they were seeing the same truths.

This little verse from Titus contains some of the elements of that common faith. "Grace, mercy, and peace, from God the Father and the Lord Jesus Christ our Saviour." Three "articles of faith" are here without which Christianity is not Christianity, and the Church is not the Church.

I—   *Article 1:* **God is the Father.** He is the One who gives us life and the One to whom we are accountable for life. Being a Christian means recognizing God as Creator and Sustainer of all existence. Verse 2 speaks of a promise God made "before the world began." The world had a beginning, but God is eternal. This vast universe is the product of His creative will, of His love, wisdom, and power.

In Paul's day a man who prated of eternal matter and denied divine creation would not have been labeled a Christian. Anyone today who explains the world without positing God as its origin is not a Christian either. He may bear the label, but what does that prove? You can sew a Hart, Schaffner, and Marx label on a pair of homemade britches. God is the Father, the Life-Giver, the Creator of the world and of man.

II—   *Article 2:* **Jesus Christ is Lord and Savior.** Belief in God as Creator is not uniquely Christian. Had the early Christians stopped there, they would not have been persecuted by Jews and Romans. What put the saints among the lions was their belief concerning Christ. To them He was the one and only Lord and Savior. He alone could redeem from sin and reconcile to God.

To tag Jesus as a man only, even a good man, a great prophet, a superlative religious teacher, would have caused little offense then, just as it causes very little now. But Jesus is Lord and Savior; life, death, and resurrection are God's mighty saving acts. If you did not believe that, you were not a Christian then, and neither are you today.

A book about Jesus bears the title *Rabbi J.* That's as far as the writer's faith extended. The resurrection would never have occurred had Jesus been simply Rabbi J. God declared Jesus to be Lord and Christ by raising Him from the dead. Nothing less is truly Christian.

III — *Article 3:* **Grace, mercy, and peace are received through Jesus Christ.** Grace is God's kindness toward us, "not by works of righteousness which we have done," but by the "renewing of the Holy Spirit" (see Titus 3:5). And peace is the outcome of salvation—peace with God, peace with others, and peace within ourselves. All of this, Christians believe, comes to us from God the Father through Jesus Christ the Lord, and in no other way. And it is the *experience* of this grace, mercy, and peace, and not the mere confession of it, that makes one a Christian.

Well, neighbor, it's pretty clear that lots of teaching called Christian today is bearing a false ID card. Much of it is borrowed Judaism or baptized paganism. The Christian is one who confesses God as Father, Jesus as Lord and Savior, and who receives salvation as God's gift through Jesus Christ.

Let us read again the ancient, irreducible content of the "common faith" that identifies Christianity: "Grace, mercy, and peace, from God the Father and the Lord Jesus Christ our Savior."

O God, we confess You as Father. We did not just happen. You made us. O Christ, we confess You as Savior. Our sins were laid on You. Your pardoning love is given to us. We embrace that salvation and bear Your name with joy. Amen.

Facing the Facts

Open the Book of God to Hebrews, chapter 9. Do the pages of Hebrews look newer and cleaner than other parts of your Bible? It's probably the most neglected book in the New Testament, but it's chock-full of saving truth that we need to look at and live by. Let us direct our attention to verses 27 and 28.

> *And as it is appointed unto men once to die, but after this the judgment: so Christ was once offered to bear the sins of many; and unto them that look for him shall he appear the second time without sin unto salvation.*

Most of us go through life dodging issues. We are like the fellow Dickens wrote about, the "Artful Dodger." Some are expert at wriggling out of things, harder to catch than an old rat in a roundhouse. But this section of Scripture confronts us with three issues we all must face.

I — **We are all going to face the coffin.** We are going to die. When, where, and how we may not know, but die we will. "It is appointed unto men once to die."

If you make an appointment you can break it. Ask any dentist! But you did not make this appointment and you will keep it. When God calls time on you, death will come for you, ready or not. One religion claims that death is unreal, a mistake of mortal thinking. The woman who got that religion started was buried a long time ago. If death is a mistake, it was the last one she made in this world.

We will die and we know it. We are fools with a capital *F* if we do not prepare for death.

II. **Then we are going to face the court.** We are going to be judged: "After this the judgment." Trees die and that's it. Animals die and that's it. But people die and they face God to be judged.

Not much preaching is done about judgment these days. You could get the impression that God has canceled it. As sure as the Bible is true, "We shall all stand before the judgment seat of Christ" (Rom. 14:10). The dead "small and great" will stand in judgment. Our "works" and our "words" and our very "secrets" will be judged, according to Scripture (Rev. 20:12; Matt. 12:36; Rom. 2:16). What a solemn, awful day that will be.

This passage from Hebrews makes it clear that Christ is coming a second time, not to make an offering for sin, but to bring the final Judgment. From the throne of judgment the trail splits two ways, into life and death, into heaven and hell. Preparation for judgment has to be made here, before we die.

III. And that brings us to the third issue: **We are all going to face the Cross.** Christ died to save us from sin. Look at the closing words of verse 26: "He appeared to put away sin by the sacrifice of himself." And look at the opening words of verse 28: "So Christ was once offered to bear the sins of many."

The Cross confronts us with the offer of life and forgiveness and peace. There is no other sacrifice for sin, no other way to God. Only the Cross saves us from hell. The cross of Jesus Christ is God's way of atoning for sin and reconciling us to himself. Apart from God's way there is no way.

Facing the Cross you can say yes or no. You can believe or reject. The claim of the Cross is absolute and its consequence is eternal. There is no middle ground.

Say yes to the Cross and you can die in peace. Say yes to the Cross and you can face the Judgment unafraid. Say yes to the Cross and you look for the second coming of Christ in joy.

But say no and you destroy hope, forfeit life, and fling yourself to hell. This is plain talk, I know, but where our destiny is at stake, plain talk beats fancy lies.

A familiar hymn declares, "I must needs go home by the way of the Cross; / There's no other way but this." The gates of heaven are hinged upon the cross of Jesus Christ. Only the Cross bridges the chasm between sinful mankind and the holy God. Cling to that Cross, and all the raging storms of evil cannot destroy you. Refuse that Cross, and nothing and nobody can deliver you. The cross of Christ or an eternity without God—there is no other alternative.

I urge you to read this passage through again. If you are not ready to face the coffin and the court, get on your knees and plead the Cross.

O Lord, we know we are going to die and face You in the Judgment. Our only hope is Your mercy and power. We plead the merits of Your death, and we claim the promise of Your life. All other ground is quicksand. We stand upon Your righteousness alone. It is enough! Amen.

As Christ Walked

A Christian should be like Christ. The attitudes and actions of Christ should be reproduced in the lives of His followers. As our Lord, He not only commands us to follow Him, He serves as the Model for our behavior in this world. *History judges the Christian by the degree to which he is like or unlike Christ.*

The inescapable rightness and justice of this standard has been recognized from the Church's beginnings. In 1 John 2:6 we read:

> He that says he abides in him ought himself also so to walk, even as he walked.

What does it mean to walk as Jesus walked?

He walked as a man contented with God's will. Jesus was always *committed* to the will of God. He could say, "I do always those things that please him" (John 8:29). In the profoundest moral struggle of His entire life, Jesus prayed, "Nevertheless, not as I will, but as you will" (Matt. 26:39; see Mark 14:36; Luke 22:42). He was unswervingly loyal to the will of His Father, even when He knew that the price of obedience would be death.

But Jesus was not only committed to God's will, He was *contented* with it. He said, "My meat is to do the will of him that sent me, and to finish his work" (John 4:34). As food satisfies the body, so Jesus was satisfied in mind and spirit by doing the will of His heavenly Father.

Paul came to this same position. He could write from prison, "I have learned, in whatsoever state I am, therewith to be content" (Phil. 4:11). To walk as Jesus walked means "godliness with contentment" (1 Tim. 6:6), not whimpering and complaining in self-pity whenever our circumstances are difficult or dangerous.

II. **Jesus walked as a man devoted to others' needs.** In a summary statement of His mission upon earth, He said, "The Son of man came not to be ministered unto, but to minister, and to give his life a ransom for many" (Matt. 20:28). One of His earliest followers summed up the life of Jesus in these words: "He went about doing good, and healing all that were oppressed of the devil" (Acts 10:38). Jesus spent His life, and at the last sacrificed His life, in order to minister compassionately to human needs.

We ought to walk in this same way! This is how the apostles interpreted Christian duty. John writes, "Whoever has this world's goods, and sees his brother has need, and closes up his heart against him, how dwells the love of God in him?" (1 John 3:17). And James wrote, "Pure religion and undefiled before God and the Father is this, To visit the fatherless and widows in their affliction, and to keep himself unspotted from the world" (James 1:27). To walk as Jesus walked means to serve the needs of the sick, the hungry, the unsheltered, the oppressed, the imprisoned, and the disenfranchised.

The Christ who would not work a miracle to feed himself performed one to feed a hungry multitude. His life was not turned inward but outward. He did not demand service, He gave service, because He cared deeply about people. This should be a mark of all who call Him Lord.

III. **Jesus walked as a man burdened for earth's lost.** He focused the primary concern of His life in these words: "The Son of man is come to seek and to save that which was lost" (Luke 19:10). Men were lost, away from God, in bitter slavery to sin, and in danger of perishing eternally. Jesus came, like a shepherd questing for lost sheep, braving the cold, the night, and the perils of the wilderness to bring the straying ones home.

This concern for the lost should characterize His people. The heart-cry of Paul, "that I might by all means save some" (1 Cor. 9:22), should be the heart-cry of every person who follows Jesus. To walk as He walked will take us straight to lost sinners, to tell them of a Savior who can rescue them from sin and give them peace.

Compared to Jesus, our steps may be weak and faltering at the first, like those of infants learning to walk. But with growing strength and continued practice, we can learn to follow Him, walking in footsteps of love to God and service to people.

Perhaps some who read this once walked with Jesus but have turned aside and lost the way. This is the time to plant your feet once more in His footprints. You will never be happy and fulfilled in any other life-style.

Some of you may never have begun to follow Jesus. You are still lost in your sins and without peace in your hearts. He invites you to come and follow Him. Trust Him as your Savior, then take Him as your Pattern, and life will be good and glad for you!

Heavenly Father, help us who name ourselves as Christians to be like Christ. May His devotion to Your will and others' needs mark our daily walk. In His name. Amen.

God's Amazing Love

Is your Bible close at hand? Let's take a look at a very exciting chapter, 1 John 3. Now center in on verse 1:

> Behold, what manner of love the Father has bestowed upon us, that we should be called the sons of God.

Neighbor, some things simply defy description or definition. They are too big, too majestic, too beautiful to capture in words. All you can do is look at them and marvel. For example, sunset over the Pacific. Or an American Beauty rose with dew on its petals. Or the view from an Alpine peak, with sun flashing across the snow and green valleys stretching for miles below.

The love of God is like that. You can't measure it. You can't describe it. You can't analyze it. You can't define it. All the categories of thought and language break down. *Try to put the love of God into words, and those words will crawl away with broken backs. They were never invented to haul that much freight.*

John doesn't attempt it. He just exclaims, "*Behold, what manner of love.*" Stand and gaze and wonder, with your eyes bulging out and your mouth hanging open.

What manner of love! **It's a sacrificing love.** Look at verse 16: "Hereby perceive we the love of God, because he laid down his life for us." The best place from which to view God's love is the cross of Jesus Christ. The holiest and noblest life ever lived was laid down for us. The Just died for the unjust. The Sinless died for the sinful. The Son of God died for the sons of men. Think of it—and wonder and weep!

II.— What manner of love! **It's a forgiving love.** Chapter 4, verse 10 declares, "Herein is love, not that we loved God, but that he loved us, and sent his Son to be the propitiation for our sins." Propitiation—that is a jawbreaker word. John means that the atoning death of Jesus makes possible the forgiveness of our sins and our reconciliation to God. That's why he can say, "I write unto you, little children, because your sins are forgiven for his name's sake" (2:12).

III.—What manner of love! **It's a conquering love.** Look at verse 8: "For this purpose the Son of God was manifested, that he might destroy the works of the devil." The Cross was love's duel with sin. There Jesus judged sin, defeated sin, abolished sin. When we yield to His love, sin's power is broken in our lives. We are transformed. We quit the life of sin for the life of love.

IV.— What manner of love! **It's an adopting love.** "Beloved, now are we the sons of God" (3:2). We were sinners, rebels, enemies of God. But He forgave us in love, changed us in love, and He takes us into His family as children; He adopts us in love.

His pardoning and adopting love changes our relationship to *God:* "Now are we the sons of God."

And His love changes our relationship to the *world:* "Therefore the world knows us not, because it knew him not" (3:1).

His love changes also our relationship to the *Church:* "Beloved, if God so loved us, we ought also to love one another" (4:11).

This, too, is involved—His love changes our relationship to the *future:* "We know that, when he shall appear, we shall be like him; for we shall see him as he is" (3:2).

"Behold!" Look at the Cross! Look at the change it makes in life. Oh, what love! Greater than a mother's love for her child. Greater than a patriot's love for his country. Greater

105

than a doctor's love for his patients. Greater than all other loves! They are but pale reflections of this amazing divine love! It is love so high that it cannot be scaled. It is love so deep that it cannot be fathomed. It is love so broad that it embraces the whole world. It is love so long that it endures for eternity. It has been written in blood. It has been written in Scripture. Has it been written in your heart?

George Truett preached the love of God to a notorious sinner, a rough, mean, drinking man who had pistol-whipped preachers and closed down revival meetings. The people of the church thought it was a mistake. They said, "You should have preached judgment and hell to him." But the next night the man was back and heard another sermon about God's love for the worst of sinners, and that night he was soundly converted to Jesus Christ.

The same pardoning and adopting love is reaching out to you today!

Our Father, we marvel at Your love. The Cross overwhelms us. It shames our hearts, but it inspires our hope. Let it work in us until we are at last like Jesus Christ. In His name. Amen.

Jesus Destroys Sin

Have you thanked God today for the Bible? What a dark, lost world this would be without the Bible: "The entrance of your word gives light" (Ps. 119:130). As you hold the Bible in your hand, praise the Lord for it.

Read 1 John 3:1-10. Now read verse 8 aloud and listen carefully:

> *He that commits sin is of the devil; for the devil has sinned from the beginning. For this purpose the Son of God was manifested, that he might destroy the works of the devil.*

Could anything be plainer than that? Not even the nose on Pinocchio's face. If a fellow sins he belongs to the devil. A sinning religion is a devil's religion.

What is sin? Let's put the question to John, for unless we keep within his terms we won't understand his message. His answer is right there in verse 4: "Sin is the transgression of the law." *Sin is doing what God forbids or refusing to do what God commands.* And if a person goes on doing wrong and refusing to do right, he is of the devil. He is not of God.

Let's take an example. God commands, "You shall not commit adultery." If a man pleads the weakness of the flesh and keeps committing adultery, he is of the devil. He may go to church, drop $10.00 bills in the offering plate, and say "Amen" to the preaching, but his performance and not his profession tells you to whom he belongs.

Jesus, the Son of God, came to destroy the devil's works. He came to snatch sinners out of the devil's dirty clutches and make them the sons of God.

The "works of the devil" and "sin" are one and the same thing. Sin is what the devil does, what he works at, and he ought to be an expert for he's been at it "from the beginning." That's about as early as you can start a career!

If Jesus is going to rescue the sinner and destroy the devil's works, this means two experiences are possible.

One is forgiveness. *He destroys the sins we have committed by forgiving them.* Not by ignoring them, not by excusing them, not by defending them—that's what people do with their sins. Jesus forgives them, and their power to accuse and enslave is broken by His act of forgiveness.

But we need an experience of cleansing, too. The devil's works, sin, is both what we have done and what we are, both our wrongdoing and our wrongbeing. Sin is an act, but back of the act is an attitude. You cover them both when you say that sin is rebellion. Jesus came to blot out the past, but He also came to straighten out the heart.

You find John declaring this truth in chapter 1, verse 9: "If we confess our sins, he is faithful and just to forgive us our sins, and to cleanse us from all unrighteousness." *He clears away the cobwebs, but He also kills the spider.*

Jesus came "for this purpose." Jesus was not an accident looking for a place to happen. He was in the world on a specific mission, and when he returned to the Father He could say, "Mission accomplished." His death and resurrection are the merit and power by which sin is destroyed in our lives.

Have you stopped sinning? You say, I want to, I tried to, but I just couldn't kick the habit. Well, as long as the devil winds you up you'll do what he wants. But if you turn to Jesus, confess your sins, and trust in Him, you will be forgiven, renewed, and cleansed.

You don't get rid of sin by grunting and sweating and straining to overcome it. *Jesus* destroys sin, not you, not me. You get rid of sin by letting Jesus do His work for you and in

108

you. A fellow trying to save himself from sin is like a man trying to dig himself out of a hole. The harder he works the deeper he goes. Jesus is the only Savior from sin.

Hugh Gorman was a born rebel. He drank heavily and fought constantly. He was booted out of the British army, for they despaired of changing him. He was flung into prison, but that didn't change him. A Nazarene minister kept telling him, "Jesus can change your life." Gorman finally yielded to Christ. Today he is a Christian gentleman, a gospel minister, and a living demonstration of the truth of our text.

Jesus Christ can save anyone who will come to him!

O God, we want to be Your children, not the devil's. Let Jesus destroy the devil's work in us until he hasn't got a smidgen of a claim to our lives. We would be entirely Yours! Amen.

Someone's at the Door!

Have you read the Book of Revelation lately? Strange book, isn't it? In some places it's as hard to understand as a government bulletin. But there is lots of great truth in Revelation that we can grasp without difficulty. Stop now and read chapter 3, verses 14-22. Probably the best-known verse in the Book of Revelation is found here—verse 20:

> *Behold, I stand at the door, and knock: if any man hear my voice, and open the door, I will come in to him, and will sup with him, and he with me.*

Isn't that a great picture—Jesus at the door! The sad truth is, He is often less welcome than the Avon lady or the Fuller Brush man.

Why isn't He in the house?

Why is He standing outside at the door? *Because He hasn't been invited in.* He will not force himself upon us. He is a gentleman, not a burglar. He respects the privacy of your heart. He will not be guilty of breaking and entering. Where He isn't wanted, He doesn't abide.

Jesus healed a demoniac once. People streamed out of the nearby villages to see what had happened. There was the once-crazed man sitting quietly at Jesus' feet, clothed and in his right mind. The demons, when evicted, had stampeded a herd of hogs down the hill into a lake where they drowned. Those foolish people saw Jesus, not as a Healer and Savior to be welcomed, but as a threat to the hog market. So they begged Him to leave, and He got into a boat and crossed the lake to the other side.

110

Jesus will not live with you uninvited. You must open the door!

II ─ Why hasn't His voice been heard?

Maybe there is too much racket in the house. You can knock at a door until your knuckles bleed, and call until your throat hurts, but if the radio is rocking and rolling, and a TV soap opera is on full blast, and the kids are screaming for Kool-Aid and cookies, and the dog is yapping at the vacuum cleaner, you won't be heard.

The same thing is true spiritually. Our hearts can be so immersed in carnal pleasures and selfish pursuits that we don't hear Jesus at the door. Our lives can be so noisy and cluttered with the hurry and worry of sin that we hear nothing but our own banging and clanging. Get quiet and think about your sins, and you will hear a hand knocking and a voice calling.

Or maybe we haven't heard Jesus because we don't want the truth about ourselves. Here in Revelation 3 Jesus had been describing a church that was affluent, proud, smug, and boasting that it needed nothing. But He jerked the wool from their eyes and said, "You are wretched, and miserable, and poor, and blind, and naked . . . repent!" (3:17, 19). Maybe we have been playing "Mirror, Mirror on the Wall" and getting the answers we want. Maybe we don't want the blunt truth from God's Word that fingers our sins and threatens our damnation. What you must risk is to admit Jesus is the Truth. Why don't we quit lying about ourselves, swallow our pride, and hear Him?

III ─ What happens if we invite Him in?

Listen to His promise: "If any man hear my voice, and open the door, I will come in." *He never stays where He isn't wanted, but He always comes where He is invited!* He wants to enter your life. He wants to be at home in your heart.

And He will share all of your life. "I will sup with him."

111

There is nothing more commonplace than supper. Jesus is not a guest for the high moments and special days of life. *He comes to be an everyday Savior and Friend.* He will share the common routines, the daily grind. He doesn't come for the occasional birthday dinner, He makes himself at home on the corn bread and cabbage days as well. He is a Savior for all seasons, and His promise is, "I will never leave you, nor forsake you" (Heb. 13:5).

Look at the closing promise in verse 21: "To him who overcomes will I grant to sit with me in my throne." Think of it! *If He sits at your table in this age, you will sit at His throne in the age to come.* Let Him share your home on earth, and He will invite you into His home in heaven.

At a camp meeting a teenager knelt at the altar of prayer. He knew next to nothing about the gospel, but he was hungry at heart for communion with God. I heard him pray in these words, "Lord Jesus, come and make a good home for yourself in my heart."

Lord Jesus, help us to knock the rust off the hinges and get our hearts open to You. Thank You for caring and coming, for standing, knocking, and calling. Come in today, come in to stay! Amen.

Last Words

Last words are often treasured. I remember a woman whose father had just died. Before his death he wrote a letter to each of his children. She read it to me with tear-filled eyes and choked voice. Her father's last words—how she valued them!

Read Revelation 21—22. They are God's last words to us in the Bible. Verse 20 of chapter 22 is a good one to underscore.

> *He which testifies these things says, Surely, I come quickly. Amen. Even so, come, Lord Jesus.*

Here is found the last promise in the Bible. "Surely, I come quickly."

Jesus is coming again! Prophets predicted His second coming. Angels announced it. Apostles proclaimed it. Throughout its history the Church has affirmed it. More important, Jesus himself declared that He would come again. He it is who says to us, "Surely, I come quickly."

The Bible is full of promises. According to Everek Storms, who personally counted them, there are 8,810 promises in Holy Scripture. Among these promises none are more precious than the promise of Jesus' return. Most precious of all are those that fell from His own lips. Shortly before His death and resurrection Jesus said to His disciples, "I go to prepare a place for you. And if I go and prepare a place for you, I will come again, and receive you unto myself; that where I am, there you may be also" (John 14:2-3). And Jesus also said, "Behold, I come quickly; and my reward is with me, to give every man according as his work shall be" (Rev. 22:12).

Everyone does not regard the promise of His coming as precious, for Christ is coming to judge the world in righteousness and truth. He is coming to reward all men according to their works. For those who have followed Him, His reward is a place in the holy and happy society of heaven: "Blessed are they that do his commandments, that they may have right to the tree of life, and may enter in through the gates into the city" (v. 14). Those who have rejected Him and have continued in their sins will be barred from heaven: "Without are dogs, and sorcerers, and whoremongers, and murderers, and idolaters, and whosoever loves and makes a lie" (v. 15).

Whether we are ready or not, Jesus is coming. His word is His bond, and He says, "Surely, I come quickly." Surely and suddenly He will appear, bringing all the traffic of time to a screeching halt, and summoning all the world before His throne of judgment.

The last promise in the Bible is followed by the last prayer in the Bible: "Even so, come, Lord Jesus." The coming of Jesus is not the dread of the Church, but its hope. The message of His coming again is not intended to frighten, but to comfort. When Paul spoke of the Second Coming, of the resurrection of the dead, of the eternal reunion of saints and their union with Christ, he added, "Wherefore comfort one another with these words" (1 Thess. 4:18).

John found comfort in his hope. He was eager for the end of evil's sway over the world, which had soaked it with blood and filled it with misery. Therefore he could respond to our Lord's promise with a fervent "Amen." From his forward-looking soul arose the cry: "Even so, come, Lord Jesus." It was the prayer of a man who could frame a great doxology in the midst of his sufferings: "Unto him that loved us, and washed us from our sins in his own blood, and has made us kings and priests unto God and his Father; to him be glory and dominion for ever and ever. Amen" (Rev. 1:5-6).

Do you look forward in hope to the return of Christ? Does your heart thrill to the promise of His coming again? If not, why not? Is it because you are not prepared to hail His coming with joy, because you have not forsaken your sins and put your trust in Him? Are you just playing religion and substituting moral respectability for vital, biblical Christianity? If you will break with sin and trust in Jesus as your Savior, you will find your heart increasingly attracted to His return as the only satisfying goal of human history and personal life.

Only one verse remains in the Bible after this last promise and prayer, the benediction: "The grace of our Lord Jesus Christ be with you all. Amen." How superbly fitting! It is the grace of our Lord that saves us from sin and enables us to clutch the promise of His coming to our hearts as comfort and hope, replying to it with the prayer, "Even so, come, Lord Jesus."

Lord Jesus, that is our prayer today! Come! Usher in Your kingdom of righteousness and peace. Reign forever! Amen.